UNSEEN JUNGLE

The Microbes That Secretly Control Our World

Eleanor Spicer Rice, PhD
illustrated by Rob Wilson

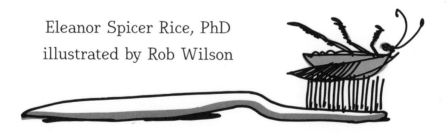

≡ mit Kids Press

For GSR, TCR, LCA, CDA, LAS, and JWS,
who always look for unseen jungles
ESR

For Maisie, who continues to inspire the best adventures
RW

Text copyright © 2023 by Eleanor Spicer Rice, PhD
Illustrations copyright © 2023 by Rob Wilson

The MIT Press, the ≣mit Kids Press colophon, and MIT Kids Press are trademarks of The MIT Press, a department of the Massachusetts Institute of Technology, and used under license from The MIT Press. The colophon and MIT Kids Press are registered in the US Patent and Trademark Office.

First paperback edition 2023

Library of Congress Catalog Card Number 2022908175
ISBN 978-1-5362-2646-1 (hardcover)
ISBN 978-1-5362-3286-8 (paperback)

23 24 25 26 27 28 APS 10 9 8 7 6 5 4 3 2 1

Printed in Humen, Dongguan, China

This book was typeset in Youbee.
The illustrations were created digitally.

MIT Kids Press
an imprint of Candlewick Press
99 Dover Street
Somerville, Massachusetts 02144

mitkidspress.com
candlewick.com

Contents

Introduction

Get used to it. You're surrounded. And covered. And filled. Unless you and everything around you just had a disinfectant shower, pretty much every square millimeter (that's a really small space; a sesame seed on top of your hamburger bun is one millimeter thick) that surrounds you has hundreds of microbes hanging out, living their best lives, having tiny conversations, arguments, buffets, you name it.

Even though we can't see them, microbes impact our lives and our world in big, beautiful, and sometimes creepy ways. Yes, some can make us sick (hi, strep throat!), and others can be associated with lots of ick (poop, for example, is packed with 'em). But without microbes living on, in, and around us, we wouldn't be able to digest our food properly, would smell funny, and could get sick or depressed or experience lots of other terrible things.

The little guys aren't just for us big folks. Microbes help loads of life-forms, from houseflies to houseplants, have happy lives. Well, some microbes help with the happy. Others are capable of mind control, gut liquefaction, and all sorts of weird, supercool deeds.

Because microbes live pretty much everywhere, you're surrounded by an invisible world of joy and drama. While you're reading this, it's possible some houseflies nearby have been turned into zombies by a fungus, mice have been mind-controlled by a protist into calling cats to come play, and a microbe party in your bottom is producing

a monster SBD*. Let it fly and thank the little guys. Unless you're in class. If that's the case, sorry about that.

In this book, you'll get a close-up view of the enchanting, thrilling microbe dramas happening right now. Like, in your yard. Or in your house. Or *in you*. But first, allow us to introduce you to microbes.

A **microbe** is any living creature that's too small to see. For most of us, anything that's half the width of a human hair (that means less than .5 millimeters) is undetectable by our eyes. That includes most bacteria (there are a couple of bacterial whoppers you can see with the naked eye, but scientists usually include those as microbes, too, just so they won't feel left out), fungi, protozoa, archaea, algae, and some tiny animals. Some scientists say viruses don't count as microbes because they don't meet the official

---

*Silent But Deadly. As in, when one breaks wind. As in, a fart.

definition of living (viruses don't grow and they don't eat). Other scientists say, "Let viruses join the party!" In this book, we're going to let a couple of viruses join the party, only because what they do to people is so out there we want you to know about them.

Let's break it down so you can see what makes up each kind of microbe.

Bacteria are single-celled creatures that come in all shapes and sizes (many variations of small). They keep their DNA tangled up in something called a nucleoid instead of having a nucleus like our bodies' cells have. DNA is a chain of chemicals that holds instructions for all sorts of traits that creatures have and will

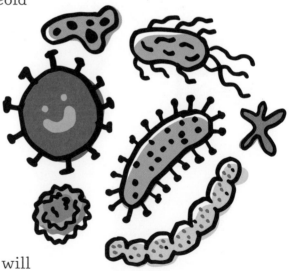

pass on to future generations. These instructions include traits for how a creature will act, how it will look, and how its body will work. Some bacteria can make us sick, but plenty more make the world a pretty sweet place to live.

Fungi. (Fungi is plural. When it's just one, it's called a fungus.) You know why everybody wants to hang out with Mr. Mushroom?

Because he's such a fun-gi! Get it? Fun-gi? Fun guy? Anyway, seriously, fungi are fun. They can have one cell or many cells, but what unites them is that their cell walls are made of chitin (unlike plants, for example, which have cellulose walls). In addition to mushrooms, you know more than one fungus among us. Yeasts are a type of fungus. Lots of molds are fungi.

Protozoa. These scooter tooters may be only one cell each, but they can move around and eat stuff.

Archaea are a lot like bacteria, except when you look inside them, their cells don't have nuclei. They're our ancient, X-treme microbes. They hold the records for surviving in the hottest places (235°F/113°C), crazy-acidic spaces, and spots where there's no oxygen, like parts of our digestive tract.

Algae are in lots of places, but you probably know them as that gunky junk floating around on ponds. Algae are sort of like if a bacterium and a plant cell got married and had babies. They're similar to bacteria in form, but they use chlorophyll like plants do to make energy.

Super-tiny animals. You have mites that live on your forehead and crawl across your face at night, looking for mates. Don't freak out. That's just the way it is. Plenty of tiny critters crawl around the planet. Take little creatures called tardigrades (sounds like TAR-duh-grades), for example. Some people call them water bears because up close they look like squishy caterpillar-bear things. They have been shipped into space and can survive all sorts of wild "I didn't think of that" scenarios, like being totally dried out for thirty years. Rock on, baby bears. You're amazing.

Viruses. Again, some say let's include them in the microbe merrymaking; others say skip 'em. Viruses are basically globs of proteins without brains (or any organs at all). They manage to

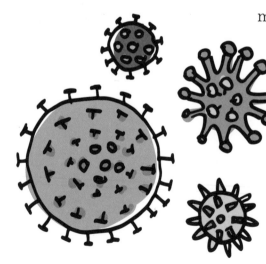

make their way into cells and use the stuff of those cells to make more and more and more of themselves. Then they burst forth and move on to their next victims. Don't think about it too long. It's kind of a brain bender. And also a little scary.

One more thing you need to know about before you read on is something called the **microbiome**. The microbiome is all the microbes (microscopic critters like bacteria and fungi) that live on and inside something. Each fly has its own microbiome bouquet. And so do you. And so does that weird dog that seems like it's always giving us the stink eye when we're just trying to walk down the sidewalk. And so does your grandmother's rosebush. And so does that pencil you chewed the eraser off of at school. Everything.

Part I
House

You may not be able to see microbes with the naked eye, but if you know where to look, you can find signs of them on and in the creatures around your house. Sometimes they'll help a body out. Other times? Well, turn the page to uncover some of your home's wildest secrets.

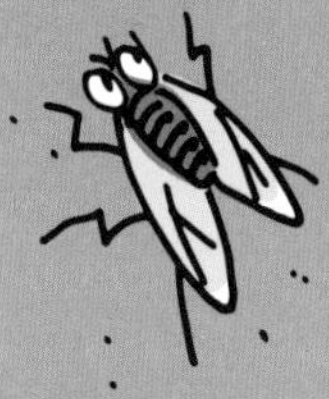

Flight of the Living Dead

Houseflies: the garbage collectors of our natural world. Born in poop, trash, and dead things, they spend their youths happily slurping away at the stuff that makes us queasy. After all, a housefly would gladly trade a slice of pizza for a dookie sandwich any day of the week. It takes serious guts—literally—to eat a dookie sandwich without getting sick. Humans couldn't do it.

But houseflies have digestive systems packed with helpful microbes that keep them as hearty as a garbage gobbler can be. That means stuff that can send our stomachs spinning, like *E. coli* bacteria, which causes food poisoning in humans, is just food to a housefly.

The microbiome on a fly's insides is basically the same across all houseflies, but the microbiomes on the outsides of their bodies can change based on where and how they live. And houseflies can live pretty much anywhere. The flies rolling around in the dead raccoons on the side of the highway host a different pack of life than the ones scarfing down garbage behind the takeout restaurant.

Even though houseflies are gracious hosts to an abundance of microbes, there's one fungus they'd rather not have around. That fungus is called *Entomophthora muscae* (say it with us one time: IN-tuh-MOF-thor-uh MUSS-kay). If one tiny spore of this dreaded fungus lands on a fly, the poor fly is in for a terrible week of first having its organs gobbled while it's alive, followed by having its mind controlled, and capped off with a spectacular death. *Entomophthora muscae* would rank at the top of a fly's most-feared list—even above flyswatters. From now on, let's call it the zombie fungus.

Here's what happens. A housefly, let's call him Gary, is minding his own business. After a nice fall afternoon of flying around your yard, searching for the sludge that seeps from garbage cans, he lands on your doorframe to take a break. He feels something land on him from above—something small, smaller than a grain of sand. No big deal, so he keeps on keepin' on. Gary has no idea that he has just become a victim of the zombie fungus.

Once it lands on Gary, the zombie fungus gets to work by making a special fungus tube that drills through Gary's body until it hits gold. Well, green, in this case, as Gary's insect blood is a green liquid called hemolymph (this one's fun to say: HEE-moh-limf). Once the tube reaches hemolymph, the zombie fungus sends its army of zombie fungus cells through the tube and into sweet, unsuspecting Gary's body. There, the fungus cells grow roots called hyphae, which work their way through Gary, digesting his organs while he is still alive. Gary struggles with the day-to-day life of a fly, not realizing his insides are getting liquefied and turning into zombie food.

Just before Gary can't stand it anymore, or before he can't *stand* anymore because the muscles that help keep him upright have trans-formed into zombie fungi, the fungi reach their long, fingerlike cells into his brain. There, they control his behavior, forcing him to land on something he likes, like that old doorframe from a week ago, and to crawl upward.

If Gary had any memories, he might think of the unlucky day he sat on that doorframe back when he wasn't a zombie. He might remember seeing another fly sitting above him that day, just as he sits above other resting flies now. He might realize that the tiny something that landed on him fell from the fly above him. But by now, Gary's mind is gone. He is merely a fly-shaped vehicle driven by a zombie fungus.

Once Gary climbs high, the fungus makes him spread his wings, airplane-style, as he clings to his favorite resting spot, perched above other houseflies like him. Then the zombie fungus gets to work. It pushes spores out from between Gary's swollen segments and ejects them so they fall like a terrifying snow before he dies. Because Gary's wings are spread wide, the spores can use them like big slides to tumble down. The wings work like a funnel in reverse— the spores spill from the small body of the fly, pour over the wings like a waterfall, and land on flies resting below. Then the cells of the *Entomophthora muscae* fungus begin the cycle all over again, gobbling up new fly bodies, turning flies into zombies and fly guts into more fungus.

Buttfiti

Have you ever noticed that sometimes the graffiti you see on lampposts or subway walls looks like a symbol or signature? That graffiti is called a tag, and it's the artist's way of signing their name to let others know they've been there. Your cat likes to leave its own calling card, too, except instead of spray paint, it uses butt juice. Or "anal gland secretions," as your vet would say. Dogs have anal glands, too, and so do a bunch of other mammals. But for now, it's feline time.

When your cat poops, it squeezes out a little bit of anal gland juice to add an extra smell. This smell says, "This is MY poop, folks! MINE and MINE ALONE! Because I was here and THIS IS WHERE I POOP." If someone else's cat comes sniffing around, it'll smell that poop tag and get the message. The sniffer will check out the p-mail (that's like email except it's poop) and realize it's in another cat's territory. By leaving a poop tag, the pooper lets strangers know they need to move along and find their own place to live, play, and eat. Move on and poop somewhere else, sniffer! And while you're at it, don't eat any of Poops McGroops's birds or food! Where does the special smell come from? Microbes living in your cat's anal glands.

Like almost every creature on the planet (including you!), every cat has its own unique microbiome. Garfield's is different from Felix's. Grumpy Cat's is different from Keyboard Cat's. Some microbes they pick up from their mamas when they're born, and others depend on what they eat, how old they are, and whether they are healthy or not. Their anal sacs have hundreds of species of microbes, working together to produce volatile organic compounds (a.k.a. stuff that smells). The number of individuals from each species present, as well as the number of *different* species present, varies from cat to cat. That means the smell they make as a group varies from cat to cat. By working together, these microbes create a special blend that becomes your cat's signature—its own work of art.

The Diggity on Dogs

When humans began keeping dogs as pets, about 20,000 years ago, we built our friendship by sharing stuff like warmth, food, safety, and sleeping spots. What a nice arrangement for us all! Today, we share more than the bare necessities, and more even than long walks and a lifetime of love and understanding. We share microbes!

Here are a few things we know about that:

1. People living with dogs have their own little microbial family in common with their pups. In other words, they have more microbes in common with *their* doggies than with other people's pups.

2. Couples who live with a dog share more microbes with each other than couples who live together and don't have a dog. One thing they share? A type of bacterium called Betaproteobacteria, found in dog slobber and on human skin! PUPPY KISSES!

3. There are many microbes that dogs and humans don't share. Dogs have different types of microbes than humans because they don't take as many baths as we do. (Or they shouldn't. Please take more baths than your dog does. Doing this can help increase your popularity at school.) Dogs are also known to

delight in a few things that most of us don't do too often, like running barefoot through the city. Snacking on cat poop. Rolling around in the mud and waiting for you to congratulate them. In all their habits, they pick up more dirt-and-cat-poop-and-mud-puddle-type microbes.

4. Country dogs have fewer allergies than city pooches. Researchers think that's because Farm-Fresh Fido gets exposed to more health-giving microbes than Big-City Biscuit.

5. When dogs eat more people-like diets, their poops are smaller than when they eat regular dog food. They've spent thousands of years taking food from us, and scientists think dogs' gut microbes digest more of the people food than puppy chow (= less waste!). "Bring out the steak!" says Lulu. Lulu, that could get expensive.

Keep Your Pets Close and Your Microbes Closer

An Interview with Hein Min Tun

This is Dr. Hein Min Tun. Here is a mathematical formula to describe him:

MICROBIAL KNOW-HOW + THE COOLEST ANIMALS
+ SAVING THE DAY = DR. TUN

He's an assistant professor at the School of Public Health at the University of Hong Kong, and he really knows how to get into the things that get under your skin.

As a public health veterinarian, he has studied the microbes of many creatures, including:

- Red pandas
- Cats
- Emus
- Giant pandas
- Chickens
- Pigs
- Humans

Definitely in the running for coolest (and fuzziest) job ever. You can do this sort of stuff, too, if that's what you decide you want to do.

While exploring the inner lives of some of our most adorable animal friends, Dr. Tun kept getting asked the same question by different pet owners. People getting ready to have babies wanted to know if they should keep their pets around. Would having Dirty Dan the Dog be unhealthy for their future squeaky-clean li'l pooper? Dr. Tun decided to find out.

"For decades, we have known that children growing up with pets have lower rates of asthma than those who do not," Dr. Tun says. So he studied the microbes of babies from pregnant and nursing women who had pets and those who did not have pets. He found that infants with pets had a few interesting microbes that infants without pets did not have.

"One microbe we found in infants who had pets, *Ruminococcus*, is linked to lower rates of allergies in children," he says. "Another microbe we found, *Oscillospira*, was relatively unknown and is reported to promote leanness."

So Dirty Dan can help make you a lean, not so mean, not sniffly machine? We'll take your word for it, Dr. Tun.

How do infants come in contact with these pet microbes?

"Pets can directly transfer the beneficial microbes to infants," like when they lick or rub the baby, Dr. Tun explains. Or they can leave microbes on indoor surfaces and in the house dust for the baby to pick up.

And since we know we share microbes with our furry friends, it makes sense that mamas can also give pet microbes to their little ones.

As babies grow, their microbial ecosystems mature from the few they have when they were born into the flourishing jungle they have as adults. Dr. Tun says these early-life microbes can be the key to a healthy jungle.

"The infant's immune system co-evolves with their gut microbial ecosystem," he says. "The gut microbes train the baby's immune cells to recognize what is friend and what is foe in the intestine. This interaction between the immune system and microbes is required for a healthy immune system."

Dr. Tun says that changes in this "microbe friend-making" process can lead to allergies and obesity later in life.

He also says it's possible that, one day, we could harness puppy power with pregnant people to help prevent future allergies in babies. But for now, the main thing to know is that it's okay to keep your pet if your family's expecting a baby— at least as far as microbes are concerned.

We can't wait to find out what Dr. Tun will discover next. Hopefully it will involve encouraging us to get more pets.

Don't Approach the Roach

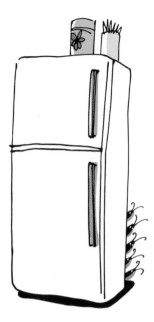

When you turn on the light at night and spot a frightening disease spreader scuttling impossibly fast to hide under your refrigerator, it is hard to believe that most of the more than 4,500 cockroach species in the world are pretty great. They eat only a few things, like bits of leaves or wet wood, and spend their days blissfully out of human sight, squeedling around forests, helpfully keeping their ecosystems happy and healthy. Thanks, roaches. (Did we just say that?!)

But then there are the *other* fellas. The very few. The Grossy McGroos who seem to have the full-time jobs of following people around and freaking us out.

Of the thousands of beneficial cockroach species on the planet, about thirty are pests. Pests are plants or animals that bother humans. Pests can cost us money, or they can disrupt the balance of our world, or they can hurt us or make us sick. Cockroach pests do all those things. These pests give the massive number of helpful roaches, roaches we never see but should definitely send thank-you notes to, a bad name. Because pest roaches are the roaches we know best, the ones that suddenly appear on the wall late at night, their creepy antennae waving at us as if taunting us, telling us they secretly take disgusting sips from our toothbrushes. They may be nasty, but we've got to hand it to them: cockroaches can be remarkably adaptable. Thanks to their microbes, pest roaches can live *anywhere* and eat pretty much *anything.* (Yes, they can even take sips from your toothbrush. Really.)

A roach's first bacterial buddy comes from its mama, who lovingly drenches her eggs with a healthy dose of a microbe called *Blattabacterium* (that's BLA-tah-back-TEE-ree-yum) before she fertilizes them. The *Blattabacterium* scoots into the baby roach's fat cells and helps it make food for the rest of its life.

Like flies, roaches can eat lots of stuff that would make other creatures sick—or even kill them. Whether it's a pile of poison or a mountain of manure, a roach can scarf it down and turn it into energy for making more roaches. Their gut bacteria help them detoxify the nasty stuff, turning toxic trash into digestible, tasty treats. German cockroaches, one of the most abundant and foul creatures in people's homes across the world, even have bacteria that can detoxify the insecticides we spray to kill them. They are like superheroes—at least to the other bugs people try to kill. To us, they're more like tiny, unstoppable, disgusting machines.

Meanwhile, back in the woods, helpful roach species probably have *Blattabacterium* but don't have the diverse microbes of the pests we know the bests. Non-pest roaches can't eat all that gross stuff pests thrive on, so they stick to the life they love,

the one as far from us as they can get, rockin' in the free world.

Pest roaches' bacterial ability to remain undefeated isn't all bad for us, though. As we humans heat up our race to use antibiotics to beat bacteria that make us sick, roaches, which can live in the most polluted environments, harbor bacteria in their guts that are helping us uncover new and useful antibacterial chemicals. We're working to use their microbes to make lifesaving drugs. That's one way to turn lemons into lemonade.

Fart as if the Future of the Human Race Depended on It

Let's talk about some Very Important Farts. Those would be termite farts, which produce 1 to 3 percent of the annual emissions of methane, a greenhouse gas more potent than carbon dioxide. That's right; the stuff that cars and factories belch out is also in termite farts. We know what you're thinking. "First they chew up my house, *then* they poot up the planet?! Why don't we dump the chumps?!" We'll tell you why: without termites, the world as we know it would end.

Humans, no matter where we live, depend on rain forests to gobble up our carbon dioxide and turn it into at least a third of the oxygen we breathe. We also need these ecosystems to add fresh water into our global water cycle. Rain forests (and other forests, like the ones near you, and non-forest places, like African savannas) depend on termites to keep the soil moist, serve as food for other animals in the ecosystem, add nutrients back into the earth so plants can grow, turn dead plants into dirt, and more. But termites wouldn't be able to get the job done without their power farts, which hint at some serious diges-tion, courtesy of their gut microbes. The future of our species depends on some tiny tooters and the microbes that make them run.

Termites have been around since the days of the ole *Brachiosaurus* (that's before *T. rex* hit the planetary scene) and evolved from their close cousins, cockroaches. Like cockroaches, they can eat cellulose. Cellulose is a compound that helps build cell walls in plants, like trees and grass. The earth has lots of trees and grass, so it has a lot of cellulose. Cellulose is the most abundant organic compound on earth. Wouldn't it be great if we could turn that into food? Yes, it would. The trouble is, cellulose is also really tough to break down, and most creatures (including humans) can't digest it. It's formed from lots of complicated and strong chemical bonds, and only a few microbes can break those bonds. Microbes like bacteria, archaea (which, if you remember, are like bacteria, except they don't have nuclei), and protozoa (single-celled creatures that can sometimes scoot around).

Termite tummies are packed with microbes that turn dead trees from indigestible dump heaps into all-you-can-eat buffets of paradise. These microbes release enzymes that hit cellulose in its sweet spots, breaking it up into sugars and other chemicals, like vinegar, that fuel termites. Termites actually have so many microbes that some termite species have microbes living *inside* other microbes that help those microbes digest the things they're helping the termite digest. Imagine a nesting doll of creatures, all working together to get the job done. These microbes are so important to termite survival that one of the first tasks of newly emerged baby termites is to eat the microbe-packed poop of their older nest-mates. As it makes its way through the digestive tract, the poop is like a packet of microbial seeds that gets planted in the baby's guts. The microbes grow into tiny but complicated ecosystems as the termite feeds them with cellulose from the plants it chomps down. This chomping down is what makes the planet run smoothly for us humans.

The termite feeds its microbes, and, in return, the microbes feed the termite. And a little gas gets released in the process, signaling a job well done on the cellulose-busting front. Termites: saving the planet one fart at a time.

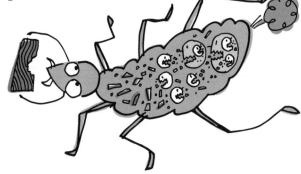

Sleep Tight, Don't Let 'Em Bite!

Like them or lump them, vampires have it pretty rough. For example, they rarely have friends because they're always trying to bite people. Also, they can't go out in the daytime, so when do they run their errands? And sure, some can turn themselves into bats, but look at their menu: blood, blood, blood, all night long. No spaghetti. No fries. No boiled eggs or zombie houseflies. The poor monsters don't even get the bottom-of-the-barrel punishment food: canned asparagus. After hundreds of years of blood meals, they probably dream of canned asparagus like we dream of buttery popcorn at the movies or a fruity popsicle on a hot day. With that diet, no wonder Dracula was so pale. Where are the vitamins? The minerals? He could have taken a lesson from bedbugs and packed his digestive tract with a bunch of microbes.

Bedbugs are about the size of apple seeds when they're fully grown, and they spend their days huddled in hiding places with their bedbug buddies, close to their nighttime party spots. They like the nooks and cracks in your bed frame, for example, or the creases between your mattress and box spring. Like most of us, they don't really like to travel too far to party and usually try to stay within 8 feet (2.4 meters) of their meals. By meals, I mean us. Our blood. To bedbugs, we humans look like tremendous sacs of blood. Well, they can't really see that well, so

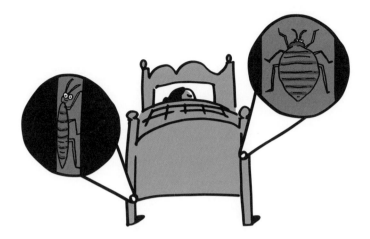

we *smell* like tremendous sacs of blood, which we kind of are. That would be like us smelling a giant chocolate bar when we are really, really hungry. We'll get to the bloody part in a minute. First, a brief ode to the many features of bedbug microbiomes, in limerick form.

> There once was a bedbug named *Cimex*
> (SIGH-mex).
> She didn't want roses or lilacs.
> If she found a good mate,
> she'd get stabbed on her date,
> and her microbes would change from her
> love's whacks.

Okay, what we're saying is that, when bedbugs mate, the male just stabs the female in the abdomen with his pointy mating thing, called an aedeagus (say it: AY-dee-AY-gus). And when he does that, he also changes her microbial community.

Another:

> **There once was a home of bedbugs**
> **who made themselves comfy and snug.**
> **They'd cuddle up close**
> **to their human host,**
> **sharing microbes with each little hug.**

So the truth is, bedbugs share microbes with their human hosts, and the humans share their own microbes with the bedbugs. We'll put this in the TMI category for the time being. As if we could ever have TMI about *anything*. No such thing as too much information, children of the world. Keep wondering and looking for more.

One last one:

Be careful with bedbugs at home.
We've sampled your dusty genome,
and from bedbugs we've found
all blowing around
are microbes, a sneezy biome.

Here's the deal: Bedbugs can cause allergic reactions, not just from biting people, but from their shed skin and poop and whatnot that they leave around the house. When entomologists took a close look at the dust floating around an infested house, they detected changes in the home's microbiome. If you can wipe out the bedbugs in your house, all those ookie bedbug microbes wafting through the air you breathe go away, too, over time.

Back to the blood meal. As Dracula and vampire bats and other blood buddies know, blood may be delicious (to some) but not so nutritious.

Think about it. Blood vs. pizza. With pizza you have cheese, which has calcium and other valuable nutrients; tomato sauce, which, thanks to a United States president in the 1980s, counts as a vegetable; dough; and all the stuff you like to put on top of it—if you're more of a "supreme" kind of pizza eater. There's plenty in a pizza to keep your body humming happily along. Now take a meal of blood. All you get in blood is a bunch of blood. That's blood cells and water, basically. Bedbugs need to get nutrients from *somewhere*. I bet you can guess where they get them. Yep. The microbes that live in their guts.

Bedbug mamas give their babies a special group of gut bacteria, including *Wolbachia* (this one's fun to say: wall-BAH-kee-yuh), before they're born (or, you know, before she lays the eggs that they hatch from). These bacteria use enzymes to help transform a bedbug's boring blood meal into all the vitamins and minerals bedbugs need to keep them creeping up on you at night. After filling themselves with your blood, they grow by 50 percent and weigh 200 percent more than when they showed up to party. Without their microbes, bedbugs could eat and eat and eat, but they would still starve to death. We know this because scientists have laced living rabbits with microbe-killing chemicals and then let bedbugs have secretly toxic rabbit blood for supper. In the end, the bedbugs got bitten back, wasting away even though their bellies were full. It turns out even vampires need a bellyful of friends.

Part II

Yard

Step out on your front porch and look around. Now look *closer*. What do you see? A vast jungle made of microbial interactions? No? That's okay. We're here to help you find some of the nutty, beautiful happenings on and in your wild yard. Turn the page and let the safari begin!

Far-Out Cicadas

Listen on a summer day or night anywhere outside a noisy city, and you'll probably hear a continuous *buzz whirr whirr whirr*—the sound of cicadas. Cicadas are those big, clear-winged, buzzy-sounding, bug-eyed insects that leave their crusty brown shells along the sides of trees and houses before they fly up to the treetops to "sing" their love songs. They live in most places around the world, and there are more than 3,000 species of them. And boy, can they sing. Male cicadas have special built-in instruments behind their wings called tymbals that can buzz and click at more than 100 decibels. That's louder than a very loud motorcycle and can be heard more than a half mile away—pretty impressive for a bug the size of your thumb. Male cicadas sing so hard because they want female cicadas to think they're the loudest, most hot-to-trot fellas around.

But one microbe, a fungus called *Massospora* (all together, now: MASS-oh-spore-uh!), is cicadas' biggest buzzkill. It can cause them to lose their privates, then lose their minds. Here's what happens: *Massospora* spores hang out as specks on branches or leaves. A happy-go-lucky male cicada going about his life accidentally walks over a *Massospora* spore, and it sticks to his body. *Massospora* spores are small, and he likely doesn't realize that the moment the spore attached to his body, his fate was sealed. He will no longer be Mr. Hot Stuff Crooner. From this moment on, he will be Mr. Killing Machine Who Kills in the Worst Possible Way.

Massospora begins its cicada feast by gobbling up the guy's privates. Then it works its way across the cicada's bottom, eating the rest of him alive and replacing Mr. Cicada's parts with the fungus. After *Massospora* reaches a critical mass on the cicada's booty, it literally drives him crazy, giving him the urge to rub his bottom on everything.

And, like that annoying kid in class who picks her nose and wipes her boogers on other kids . . . Wait. Are YOU that annoying kid?! If you are, stop picking your nose and wiping your boogers on the other kids! It's gross! And don't eat those boogers, either! We know you've tried it! That is also gross! Listen to us. We know what we're talking about.

Anyway, like that annoying kid *who is certainly not you* who picks her boogers and wipes them on other kids, the cicada begins to rub his bottom on everything he can, wiping the *Massospora* hither and yon. The wiped spores wait for other cicadas to wander over them so they may begin their lives as actual butt munchers anew.

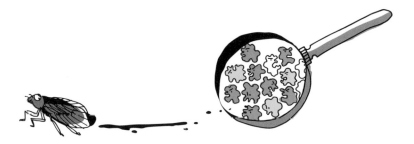

Perhaps the meanest *Massospora* maneuver is that, while it devours the male cicada's abdomen, it does not devour his tymbals, leaving him to sing his earsplitting song, luring in hopeful females. And because he has the drive to wipe his bottom on everything, as soon as an aspiring lover arrives, full of hope and promise, he can't help but greet her with a butt wipe. Instead of mating with her, he infects her with *Massospora*.

Massospora mind control gets even more devious from there. Female cicadas have this happy little wing dance they do to attract males. *Massospora* forces infected males to flick their wings in a way that looks like the female dance. When another male is tricked into flying over to meet what he thinks is a girlfriend, he instead finds a male cicada who promptly—you guessed it—gives him a big butt wipe. Life over.

As far as we know, *Massospora* infections don't spread far and wide enough to quiet our summer canopy. Instead, the spores skulk around on surfaces and in cicada bottoms just enough to keep their creepy cycle going.

Don't Tell Mom the Babysitter's (Almost) Dead

Ladybugs are a type of beetle, garden buddies who gleefully prey on creatures that munch our pretty plants. They're like cheerful lions among the leaves. Their bright red color and spots warn would-be predators, like birds, not to eat them because they taste terrible. Because no animals are interested in eating them, and because people encourage them to stick around in their gardens, you'd think ladybugs would have a one-way ticket to Easy Street, wouldn't you? Well, you would think wrong.

Out in the garden flies a tiny wasp, an orange-and-black insect with green eyes. Its scientific name is *Dinocampus coccinellae*, but here we're calling it a green-eyed wasp because that's what it is. It cruises through the vegetation, beady eyes searching for bright red bodies. This wasp is smaller than a ladybug but has a way of making a beetle's life miserable. It all begins with body snatching.

A green-eyed wasp mama is small, and her babies are smaller. Wasp babies look like little squishy tubes, with mouth holes at one end and butts at the other. No stingers. No legs. They're pretty defenseless. Life could get rough for a little wasp grub, alone in this world.

Don't worry, grubbers. Mama wasp has a plan. A dastardly plan.

A mother green-eyed wasp looks for ladybugs in the leaves. When she finds one, she lands on him (ladybugs can be boys or girls; this one happens to be a boy) and inserts her stinger (which is really just a pointy straw for laying eggs) into the ladybug. She lays a single egg inside him and takes off. The ladybug is all like, "Whoa! Whawazzat?!?!?!" but nothing much seems amiss, so he keeps going about his buggy business.

Meanwhile, a wasp baby hatches inside his abdomen and swims around, gobbling up the ladybug's living tissue. As it swims, it infects the ladybug with a special virus it brought along when its mother injected it into the ladybug. The virus makes its way to the ladybug's brain and reproduces there.

Here we have the ladybug, a wasp baby growing in his bottom, viruses replicating in his top. The ladybug possibly feels a little funny, but he isn't dead. When the wasp gets big enough to pupate, it needs to do so outside the ladybug. This is when things get weird. Or weirder.

The ladybug starts acting strange. He clings to a stalk or a leaf like he's in battle and has to hold the front line. He stops walking and just clings. Then the wasp bursts forth from the ladybug's body, but it doesn't kill him. Instead, the wasp crawls under his protective ladybug legs, and the ladybug hovers over it, guarding it from anybody who may come near with defensive twerking in the offender's direction.

Scientists think the virus wasn't doing too much harm while the wasp was growing inside the ladybug. But when the wasp made its way into the great outdoors, the virus burst cells in the ladybug's brain. The result was total ladybug mind control, which caused the ladybug to grip the stem tightly with his toes and to behave defensively. The virus turned the ladybug into a full-time babysitter for the creature that just spent its entire life gobbling his ladybug insides.

The ladybug stays in bodyguard mode until the wasp emerges from its cocoon as a fresh-faced, grown-up green-eyed wasp, ready to mate and find more ladybugs to infect with its babies. When it flies off, the wasp takes along some mind-control virus to add to the infection.

As for the ladybug babysitters, three-quarters of them die from their mind-control experience. And out of the quarter of them that recover, some even get infected again! Not the best babysitting gig, if you ask us.

Beauty Secrets of Birds

Getting as good-looking as a bird takes a lot of work. Have you ever seen a bird preen? Preening is the bird equivalent of a makeover plus a doctor's visit. The bird rubs its head gently along its feathers, pulling each quill through its beak, making itself nice and shiny. Then it fluffs up its feathers and puts them all back in place, shakes out the dust and dirt, and kicks out any creatures, like mites or lice, trying to live in its plumage. Preening also helps make birds' feathers waterproof so they can fluff around in the rain with hardly a care in the world.

As they preen, birds rub
their heads over a
special gland
on their
backs, just above
their tails, called the uropygial
(yur-uh-PY-jee-ull) gland, or preen gland. The
preen gland releases a little dab of oil to help
with that shine. This gland is also the rockin'
host of a huge microbe party, and bacteria living
there give birds secret boosts in exchange for a
feast of bird body oils.

Some preen gland bacteria work as agents
of disease destruction. When the bird smooths
bacteria and oil over its feathers, the preen
bacteria work to kill other bacteria that can
make the bird sick.

Dark-eyed juncos are cheery little sparrows
that pip and hop around North America, looking
for seeds and the occasional juicy bug or two. In
the spring, they also look for the loves of their

lives, or at least the loves of their season, to settle down, build a nest, and raise babies all summer.

When it's time to look their best, junco preen oil gives dark-eyed juncos the sheen they need. It also gives them a secret signal, thanks to bacteria living near that preen gland. These special bacteria manufacture scented compounds that act as junco perfume. As the birds spread it over their feathers, they end up smelling like a bouquet of delicious hunky bird-ness to other birds. Juncos who have thriving odor-making bacteria living around their preen glands seem irresistible to other birds, and that helps them find their sweet summer flings.

Microbes Trick the Deadliest Animal

Allow us to introduce you to the deadliest animal on the planet. Want to take a guess? A lion, perhaps? We heard hippos can get surprisingly murderous. Or maybe timber wolves. Sharks! Definitely sharks. Crocodiles and alligators combined? Nope, nope, nope, nope, and double nope. It's the mosquito. That weird-looking fly the size of your fingernail kills about a million people every year, though many of the planet's 3,000 mosquito species don't bite humans at all. People don't die because mosquitoes suck their blood. They die from mosquito bites because mosquitoes can transmit deadly diseases.

One of the deadly microbial diseases that mosquitoes transmit is malaria. Malaria is caused by a mind-altering microbe called a plasmodium* (easy enough to say: plaz-MOH-dee-yum!). But the news isn't all bad! Even though microbe-laden mosquitoes can kill, they can save lives, too.

First, the dreaded, deadly malaria. Malaria, which kills about 500,000 people each year, travels from person to person in the guts of a mosquito. And look, malaria is no picnic for mosquitoes, if it makes you feel any better. Malaria infects mosquitoes

*A plasmodium is neither bacterium nor virus. It's a single-celled creature that lives in other creatures.

just as it does humans, and it can kill them, too.
But back to people. When a mosquito infected
with the malaria parasite bites a person, it
barfs a little bit of that parasite into the human.
From there, the plasmodium is free to go crazy,
reproducing in our blood and livers, and sometimes killing us. If that isn't devious enough, the
malaria parasite has a couple of tricks up its
sleeve (no, plasmodia do not wear shirts; they
don't have arms) to ensure Madame
Bites-A-Lot Mosquito will do
malaria's dirty work.

The malaria parasite needs
humans to complete its life cycle,
and it needs mosquitoes to move it
from human to human. To make
sure it gets barfed into a
human (and not your dog, for
instance), malaria messes with
the mosquito's sense of smell,
causing the infected mosquito

to think humans are waaay tastier than other animals. Malaria-infected mosquitoes land on humans three times more than mosquitoes that aren't infected with malaria.

Okay, so now malaria has used mosquito mind control to find its human. It has reproduced and spread throughout the human's body and needs to get into someone else's body. How can it ensure a mosquito will come along so it can hitch a ride to someone else? That's malaria's second trick up the sleeve we know it does not have. Not only does malaria make mosquitoes think uninfected humans smell tasty; it also changes the way infected people smell to make them more attractive to mosquitoes. Once the malaria infects a person, it needs to get back into a mosquito so it can get carried around to infect another person. Mosquitoes have very little eyes to see but nice long antennae to smell. They mostly use smell to find their way around the world, and in particular use their sniffers to find their next meal.

Malaria causes people to smell so tasty that children infected with malaria are two times more attractive to all mosquitoes than children who aren't infected. What sneaky sneaks these plasmodia are!

But microbes and mosquitoes aren't all bad news. One microbe may be a key to helping mosquitoes spread love instead of diseases. Actually, mosquitoes won't spread love. They will always be annoying. But they may stop spreading so many diseases! The secret is a bacterium called *Wolbachia*.

Wolbachia lives in the cells of more than half the world's insects (including our bloodsucking friends the bedbugs). It's spread from mother to baby through her eggs. Now, think about this. Both male and female insects can be infected with *Wolbachia,* but only females can spread it. Imagine you are *Wolbachia,* and you want the world to have as many insects infected with *Wolbachia* as possible. You don't want uninfected females laying eggs; you only want your infected mamas having babies! How can you reduce the number of baby bugs hatching from non-infected eggs? Here's an idea: cytoplasmic incompatibility. We'll call it CI.

Here's how it works: When a female insect infected with *Wolbachia* mates and lays eggs, all her babies hatch with *Wolbachia,* whether or not the daddy was infected. BUT when a male insect infected with *Wolbachia* mates with a female insect who is not infected (and so cannot lay *Wolbachia*-infected eggs), his *Wolbachia* sperm cause her non-*Wolbachia* eggs to become infertile.

"BOOM!" says the sneaky *Wolbachia.* "No babies for you!"

In this way, *Wolbachia* slowly increases its spread in its quest for global domination.

Wolbachia has been found to do a ton of helpful tasks inside the bugs it infects, but in mosquitoes, it turns out that *Wolbachia* competes with the deadly diseases that infect them, including malaria, chikungunya, Zika, yellow fever, dengue, and more. *Wolbachia* makes it harder for these and other viruses to live inside the mosquitoes, which makes it harder for the mosquitoes to transmit them.

Right now, researchers are releasing *Wolbachia*-infected mosquitoes by the millions in towns all over the world and finding that the prevalence of some mosquito-vectored diseases is declining. Not that we would ever be glad for mosquito bites, but this may be one case where we welcome the little suckers.

How to Discover the Big Deal of Little Things

An Interview with Molly Hunter

Sometimes universities put their best brains together to form supersquads. Well, they call it "collaborating." That sounds boring. We prefer supersquad. Supersquads work together to solve especially tricky questions.

Meet Molly Hunter. Molly is part of a *Cardinium* supersquad that includes smart folks from North Carolina State University (like Manuel Kleiner), Iowa State University (like Stephan Schmitz-Esser), and Molly's own university, the University of Arizona. Their big brains basically span the whole continental United States. Not literally. Brains that big would be very hard to carry around on our tiny necks. Molly and her supersquad have regular-sized brains, as far as we know. But curious ones. Curious like you and me.

Molly's supersquad wants to know how a microbe called *Cardinium* (car-DIN-ee-yum) is able to perform Jedi mind tricks on insects. They know that *Cardinium* is a bacterium living in the reproductive organs of a ton of different species of insects, spiders, and more. (Fun fact: up to one out of every ten arthropods is infected with this bacterium. According to our calculations, that's roughly 14 gagillion arthropods. No, gagillion is not a real number.)

They also know that critters infected with *Cardinium* have this *Wolbachia*-like thing going on with their reproduction. Remember *Wolbachia*? From page 58?

Cardinium is passed from a mother bug to her children, so it is best for the bacteria if there are more girls in the world. Girls infected with *Cardinium*, that is. Say you have a wasp. (Molly's *Cardinium* supersquad studies a bunch of teeny tiny wasps of different types, all called *Encarsia*, pronounced like the fun statement: in-CAR-see-yah!). And that wasp is a girl, and she is infected with *Cardinium*. All her babies are infected with *Cardinium* because she passes it along to them when she lays her eggs. Her little daughter wasps grow up to lay *Cardinium*-infected eggs. Her sons? Well, that's where it gets extra interesting. For one, *Cardinium* can cause some kinds of *Encarsia* wasps that should have been males to turn into females. Because remember, with *Cardinium*, females rule!

There's a different kind of *Encarsia* called *Encarsia suzannae*. (Why the *suzannae*, you ask? You ask such good questions! This wasp was named after a real person named Suzanne. She's also on this supersquad and has studied these wasps a long time! Let's call the wasp Suzanne.)

If a *Cardinium*-infected male Suzanne mates with an uninfected female Suzanne, their eggs never hatch. His *Cardinium*-infected sperm kill all their potential babies! If he mates with an infected female? Babies galore. All infected, of course. And that is how *Cardinium* continues its path toward total arthropod domination.

To quote *Cardinium* supersquad member Molly:

"So it seems sometimes bacteria are kings, and we animals are just their servants!"

Serve on, little animals.

The *Cardinium* supersquad knows *what* happens, but they don't know *how* it happens. Like, what is *Cardinium* doing inside the animal's body that controls the animal's reproduction? That's what they're trying to find out.

Buckle up. Molly's about to tell you what a *Cardinium* supersquad does.

"Hi, everybody. I'm Molly Hunter. Some people call me Dr. Hunter because I have a PhD in entomology (that's the study of insects), and I work as a professor and researcher. One of the things I study is the bacterium *Cardinium*, because it's amazing. If we figure out how *Cardinium* works, we could use its power to help reduce what we call 'vector-borne diseases' for millions of people. Those are diseases like Lyme disease and malaria that are transmitted by creatures like ticks and mosquitoes. Just imagine!

"One thing we do to study *Cardinium* is to 'cure' *Cardinium*-infected insects with antibiotics.

Remember, *Cardinium* is a bacterium, and antibiotics can kill bacteria. Then we can see how these cured insects reproduce differently without their reproduction-controlling bacteria working behind the scenes.

"But we need to learn more about the switches and levers *Cardinium* pulls inside the insect to help it take control over the insect's reproduction. To do that, we have to dive deeper.

"Imagine you come with me on a trip, but to take that trip we need to shrink. Are you imagining this? Okay, we are shrinking now. First, we are the size of the period at the end of this sentence ↘.↙ That's us. That means we are the size of the wasp our team studies. Yes, some wasps are that small!

"Now, you and I keep shrinking. We are way smaller, so small we couldn't see us if we were normal-sized or even the size of the wasp. We are the size of *Cardinium*, and we can go inside the wasp and have a look around. This is one of our study wasps, and the researchers on our team have made the *Cardinium* inside this wasp glow by adding a 'glowing tag,' which sticks to the bacteria. The researchers can then use microscopes to look at the wasp's cells and see which ones are glowing. That gives us clues about what the bacteria might be doing inside the wasp.

"Let's get smaller, though. Smaller than the bacteria and wasp cells. Small enough that we can see proteins. Proteins are molecules that make the action happen inside cells. Some proteins come from the bacterium, and others come from wasp cells. When we analyze the proteins, our team can use tools to see how these proteins hook together to form patterns.

"Smaller still, and we can see bacterial DNA and RNA and wasp DNA and RNA. The DNA and RNA give instructions for how to make more proteins. We want to be able to read the instructions the bacteria give to tell the wasp proteins to do exactly what the bacteria want. We have tools to decode these instructions. For example, we can chop up the DNA or RNA into little pieces and put them into a machine that reads their instructions to us.

"In our research team, each of us adds our own tools to help crack the code. It's exciting when one of us comes back to the group with a new piece to the puzzle."

When you break the code, Molly, YOU will be able to control the bacteria, which control the insect! YOU WILL BECOME THE RULER! MWAH HA HA HA HA! Ahem. Excuse us. We got a little carried away there for a second. What we mean is that you can then work to use *Cardinium* to help control arthropods that spread disease, which can help save human lives. Thanks for telling us about your *Cardinium* supersquad!

The Very (Very) Hungry Caterpillar

Birds do it, bees do it, educated fleas probably do it, but caterpillars? If "it" is "harbor microbes," then caterpillars don't seem to get too involved. We know what you're thinking. "How can that be?! You said microbes were *everywhere!*"

We know what you're also thinking. "Caterpillars eat leaves. Leaves are made up of cellulose. You said cellulose needs microbes to break it down. And now you're telling me *caterpillars*, the *original leaf eaters*, aren't packed to the brim with microbes?! How can I ever believe anything you say again?!"

Okay, maybe you're not thinking exactly that, but we get the picture. Now hear us out.

There are nearly 200,000 species of butterflies and moths on this planet. All these winged wonders begin life as grubby little caterpillars, inching their way around the world. Most caterpillars need to eat plants, and mostly leaves, to become butterflies or moths. As you recall from reading about termites, or perhaps even from reading about cows if you skipped ahead, plants are very hard to digest, thanks to their cellulose.

Many plant-loving animals house microbes that break cellulose into nutrients they can use. Not caterpillars. They rely on inefficiency and their own enzymes. Their digestive tracts are like long, simple straws that wring out nutrients wherever they can. They have a section that is extremely alkaline (that's the opposite of acidic on the pH scale) that works to bust up leaves, and a section that squeezes whatever nutrients and water it can from the chomped- and alkalined-up leaves. Then they poop out what's left over. As a result, caterpillars can't get as many nutrients out of the plants as microbe-packed creatures can. To compensate, they just eat more. And more. And more. They make up for their digestive inefficiency with food quantity.

Still, microbes can affect caterpillars in sometimes tricky ways. One microbe, called a baculovirus (BACK-yoo-loh-vy-rus), may be the most gruesome of caterpillar contaminators. The method of caterpillar murder by baculovirus is so dreadful that if caterpillars had night terrors, the baculovirus would be the number one culprit.

Before you go feeling sorry for baculovirus-infected caterpillars, let's first meet our victims, a type of caterpillar called a spongy moth. Spongy moths are the absolute worst. A man named Étienne Léopold Trouvelot brought spongy moths to Massachusetts back in the late 1800s. He wanted to breed them with other silkworms to have his own silk-making operation in the United States. "I'm a genius!" he probably thought. Then he decided his silk-making plan wasn't actually such a hot idea and gave up on the moths. Then he accidentally let them go free. Big mistake.

Trouvelot didn't realize he'd made a big mistake. He gave up on entomology and silk making altogether and became a celebrated astronomer. He had no idea that entomologists would continue to curse his name to this day. His moths, and their voracious appetites, spread across the northeastern United States and parts of Canada and caused destruction and despair never before seen.

Spongy moths, like many caterpillar species, like to eat. A lot. They can eat more than 500 species of plants. Since the 1980s, spongy moths have defoliated more than a million acres of trees each year. One year, they defoliated more than 12 million acres of trees. Defoliate means they eat so many leaves off the trees that the trees are totally bare. The trees can't make the energy they need to survive. Whole forests can die. Today, spongy moths rank in the top 100 invasive pests on the planet, and the US and Canadian governments work nonstop to halt their spread.

Which brings us back to the baculovirus. Spongy moths eat, eat, eat in the nighttime, and in the day, they climb down the tree trunk to rest, hide, and molt. (Caterpillars, like all insects, molt, or shed their tight outer skins to reveal bigger skins beneath, in order to grow.) Baculovirus waits on the leaves for a spongy moth to eat it. When it is eaten, instead of getting pooped out quickly with the leaves, it moves into the caterpillar's endocrine system (that's the group of organs in the body that make hormones, including the hormones that help spongy moths

grow) and switches off a gene that tells the caterpillar to molt.

So rather than going down to molt in the
daytime, the infected caterpillar remains up in
the tree, gorging itself on leaves, getting fatter
and fatter, while the baculovirus releases a cock-
tail of enzymes that digest the caterpillar alive,
turning it from a fuzzy caterpillar to a black,
goopy virus soup high in the trees. Then, you
guessed it, the goopy virus soup drips down on
other leaves for other spongy moths to gobble.
Baculovirus is so great at killing spongy moths
that foresters spray it on trees in the hopes a
caterpillar will eat it. It could save millions of
acres of forests over time.

Spongy moths of the world: you've been
warned. Except you can't read if you're a spongy
moth, so really you probably haven't been
warned. And we don't want you to be warned!
Eat the baculovirus! It's tasty!

The Woman Who Gave Caterpillars Poop Transplants

An Interview with Erica Harris

This is Erica Vernice Harris. We can call her Dr. Harris. She's a postdoctoral research fellow at Agnes Scott College in Georgia. One of our favorite things about Dr. Harris is that she performed poop transplants on caterpillars during her graduate work at Emory University. That means she took poop from one caterpillar and put it into another caterpillar to see how its new poop would affect its microbes and response to parasites. Poop for science! And now she's ready to tell us what she learned.

Dr. Harris, we *just said* that caterpillars don't have too many microbes, but you study monarch butterfly caterpillar microbes. What gives?

"Like the other caterpillar species we know of, monarchs don't have many microbes in their guts. But those few microbes present are doing important work. For example, monarch caterpillars eat this plant called milkweed.

"Milkweed is famous for being toxic to many other species of insects but not to monarchs. Instead of getting sick from eating milkweed, monarch caterpillars save the toxins in their bodies to help them taste bad to hungry caterpillar-eating birds."

Does that go for all the different types of milk-weed?

"Some milkweed species, which we call 'medicinal,' are more toxic to plant-hungry creatures than other types of milkweed, which we call 'non-medicinal' species. When sick caterpillars eat the medicinal milkweed, they can be healthier than those caterpillars that eat the non-medicinal milkweed. For example, caterpillars who eat non-medicinal milkweed are more likely to be infected with parasites. Parasites can make them unhealthy. If they eat medicinal milkweed instead, the parasites have a harder time surviving in the caterpillars' bodies.

"But there's more! Caterpillars that eat medicinal milkweed species also have more microbe variety in their gut. When caterpillars poop out the milkweed, these microbes come out, too. We found that if you transplant the feces of a healthy monarch caterpillar that has been eating the medicinal milkweed into a parasite-infested caterpillar, the infested caterpillar starts to get better. That means these medicinal milkweed microbes act like medicine, too!"

Microbial poop as medicine. How did you get the healthy caterpillars' poop into the sick caterpillars?

"That's easy. We put the medicinal frass* onto the milkweed plants the caterpillars were eating. The caterpillars ate the frass along with the leaves."

So you're saying you tricked them into eating someone else's poop. All in a day's work.

*Frass is another word for insect poop. Feel free to use this against your friends and enemies.

Bring Out the Dead

From the instant you die, your microbiome begins to collapse and gives rise to a new biome: a necrobiome, which helps your body transition from a lean, mean, livin' machine into a part of the nonliving earth. In other words, certain microbes living in and around you help you to decompose. The necrobiome works at such a predictable rate that it can help medical examiners determine time of death.

But it takes more microbes to deal with the dead than just the ones on the body. Creatures who eat dead things need microbes to help break down the parts of corpses that are unpalatable to most of us. Want to hear about our favorite?

Vultures: they aren't the best-looking birds in town, but they certainly are some of the most helpful. The Great Cadaver Consumers turn dead bodies into soil-fertilizing poop. Lots of dead bodies. In some continents, like Africa and South America, vultures eat more meat than all predators combined. And thank goodness they do. Since vultures eat food that could be eaten by dead-meat-eating disease spreaders like wild dogs, they help keep terrible diseases like rabies in check.

But the thing is, carrion—a.k.a. the decaying flesh of dead animals—is toxic to most creatures.

The dead animals' necrobiomes have some tough-acting microbes that can make non-vulture stomachs extremely ill. Clostridia, for example, are super common on dead animals, and members of this bacteria group can cause deadly diseases like botulism and tetanus.

Another necrobiome favorite is the flesh-eating fusobacteria, which can, well, you probably already guessed what it can do. "Yikes!" you say? Don't be so hard on fusobacteria. While the idea of flesh-eating makes our living skin crawl, fusobacteria and other necromicrobes are doing useful work on dead animals.

While eating raw roadkill can make many beasts' stomachs turn (or much, much worse), vultures say, "No problem! We got a thing for that!"

 Vultures actually wait for necrobiomes to start decaying bodies before they tuck in for lunch. That's because these

microbes tenderize bodies and make it easier for the birds to chomp and rip putrid flesh.

Vultures' digestive systems work as "good microbe" factories. As vultures scarf down those roadside possums, their extremely acidic guts nuke the bacteria that make others sick. Their digestive tracts don't kill all microbes, though. They act as a filter to harvest helpful microbes and collect them in the vultures' intestines. There, these helpful microbes work to digest the very beings they once lived on, breaking down the dead animals and turning them into vulture vitamins. Carry on, carrion!

Part III

Food

Hamburgers, hot dogs, fruits, and veggies—most of your food either needs or battles microbes in order to make it to your plate. Take a trip to the farm, and take a look at your meal's microbial wild rides.

Bee-youtiful Bee Bowels

Oh, busy little bees! It takes guts to be a bee!
By that we mean it takes the microbes that live
in their guts for bees to survive. Yes, yes, bees
are cute enough (aside from their stingers), with
their fuzzy little faces as they bounce from flower
to flower. Yes, they help make the fruits and

vegetables that are one out of every three bites of food we eat possible. And it's lovely how the flowers give them a healthy bee diet of nectar and pollen in return. But without their special honeybee microbe bouquet, they wouldn't be able to eat that nectar and pollen at all. In fact, without their microbes, some of that nectar could be poisonous to them.

It all starts when a bee is born—or when it hatches. Its sisters feed it in the bee nursery by throwing up food into its mouth. When they barf, they give it some of the microbes that live in their own guts, and those microbes start to make their home in the little bee's digestive tract. When the bee comes out of its cell as a grown-up, it picks up even more microbes while walking around its hive.

Each hive's microbes are different because each hive's bees fly to their own suite of flowers, picking up their unique set of microbes between petals, on leaves, and anywhere else they may wander. The bees come home and blend microbes together by walking around their hive and also by the barf fest, shared only with other members of their colony. Many plants have nectar that can be toxic, but bee microbes have the antidote. These microbes break down the toxins, making the nectar digestible to our bee, their host. Bee belly bacteria don't just save the bee from poisoning, though. They also keep it from starving by breaking down other nectars and pollens into sugars and proteins the bee can use for energy. Without them, it'd be too hungry to fly.

One last thing, besides saying thank goodness for a bee's good ole germy guts: Microbes work

as a bee's immune system. Because the bee's special microbial blend loves to live on and in the bee, it fights off other microbes that might want to cause the bee harm. When a bad-actor bacterium like American foulbrood success-fully invades a bee colony and makes it sick, sometimes good beekeepers will intervene by dumping antibiotics on the hives. The thing is, antibiotics kill so many bacteria. In addition to killing American foulbrood, these medicines can destroy the bacteria that help bees eat, as well as the bacteria that keep them disease-free. When medicine does that, bees starve or get too sick to live. Sometimes the cure can cause more harm than good. They need their own sweet gang of unseen heroes to keep stayin' alive, stayin' alive.

So go on, little bee. Give those guts a high five! Or maybe don't do that. That might be gross. Just be kind to them and let that gut garden grow.

CoffeeBeetle Don'tQuit Won'tQuit

Fuzzy, brown, and a little bigger than a poppy seed: the coffee berry borer, along with its millions of fuzzy, brown, little-bigger-than-poppy-seed-sized friends, causes more than $500 million worth of damage to coffee beans a year. This beetle eats coffee beans, even though coffee beans contain one of the deadliest natural poisons to insectkind: caffeine.

Plants have been around on earth a lot longer than humans. Insects began chomping away on those plants millions of years before humans ever sat on a rock and called it a chair. During that time, plants had to adapt ways to protect themselves from all those hungry insects. Why not poison them? Many plants turn the nutrients they suck up from the soil into toxins in the hopes they will bump off eager flowermunchers before they do too much damage. Apple seeds have cyanide. Walnuts have arsenic. And coffee has caffeine.

We know caffeine because it gives us the delightful get-up-and-go many of us need to get going. But caffeine is actually a toxin. Too much caffeine can kill us. A shot of espresso? No problem. Six shots of espresso? We could have heart issues or panic attacks. A hundred or so shots of espresso? See you on the other side. Each coffee beetle, because it eats nothing but coffee beans, swallows the human equivalent of 200 to 500 cups of coffee a day and keeps on truckin'. Of course, because they're in this book, they have a secret microbial ally. But they also have something else, something they stole from bacteria millennia ago, that gives them the power to pound java and only java for their whole lives.

First, the caffeine detox. A female coffee berry borer chews her way into the fruit, called a cherry, growing on a coffee tree. She is ready to lay her eggs, so she tunnels around and finds the seeds that will become coffee beans. There, she lays thirty to fifty eggs, which hatch into little grubs that chomp away at the fruit and seeds. Her beetle babies spend

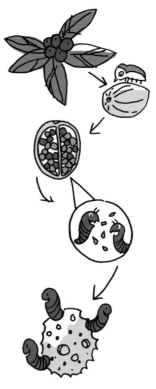

their entire grubhood in the coffee cherry. When they molt into adults, the girls mate with their brothers and then abandon them to search for more coffee beans to bite. Their brothers never see the light of day, dying in the berries where they were born.

So you see, coffee berry borers eat coffee and only coffee, but they never get the jittery joes. When researchers harvested the beetles' poop, they found no caffeine. Zip. Zero. Zilch. Nada. When the same researchers fed the beetles anti-biotics, which kill bacteria, the beetles began pooping out caffeine. This means that something was going on between the first berry bite and pooptown to remove caffeine. So the scientists harvested beetle guts, and they found, among an abundance of other microbes, a curious bacterium called *Pseudomonas fulva* (this one's a roller coaster to say: SOO-doh-MOH-nuss FULL-vuh). *Pseudomonas fulva* loves a jolt of joe more than anything else, breaks down caffeine, and turns it into nutrients beetles need to ~~ruin our mornings~~ survive.

Breaking down caffeine is only half the beetle's trouble, though. Coffee beans are high in carbohydrates. Carbohydrates are basically monster-sized molecules that can be tough to digest, especially for a little beetle. They need to be broken into smaller bits. Coffee berry borers seem to have no problem breaking up carbohydrates, thanks to a special gene called HhMAN1.

(Genes have weird names. Don't ask us why.) But HhMAN1 isn't a run-of-the-mill insect-type gene. This gene is usually found in bacteria. So what happened? Scientists think that somewhere along the line, millions of years ago, coffee berry borers *stole a gene from a bacterium and incorporated it into their own*

genome. Now, instead of asking Buddy Bacteria to bust carbs for them, they just do it themselves because Buddy's genes are permanently a part of the coffee berry borer's genome. They're like self-made, carb-crashing cyborgs, except instead of machine bits, they use bacteria bits.

Coffee farmers have a hard time trying to save their beans from these beetles. The beetles spend most of their lives *inside* the berries farmers want to protect, so they're hard for farmers to reach to squash or blast with insecticide. This means berry borers keep beating us to our java, and the destruction in their wake pushes our coffee prices up and up.

Spying on Food Microbes Is a Real Job

An Interview with Nakieta McCullum

This is Nakieta McCullum. She is a regulatory food microbiologist for the United States government. That means she checks all kinds of foods to make sure they don't have too many harmful microbes on them. In other words, it's her job to keep us from getting poisoned. So we asked her a few questions to learn some of the secrets behind her super-science superpowers.

Nakieta, what sparked your love of microbes?

"I took a microbiology course in high school and fell in love! Microbiology combined my interest in medical science and, oddly enough, my love of logic puzzles."

What's the coolest part about your job?

"Each day, I get to help keep my community safe and healthy, and I get to work in a scientific field that is always advancing. I am always learning new things about the field I love."

What can be cooler than that?!
What's your favorite microbe?

"Probably *Escherichia coli*."

The culprit behind all that food poisoning?

"Yep."

Nakieta! Why?!

"This bacterium has been studied for almost 100 years. We know a lot about it, but we are always learning more about it, too. Most people think of *E. coli* as something that makes us sick, but right now it's being used as a drug delivery system to help people get well. It also looks cool under the microscope."

Rootin' Tootin' High Pollutin'

Whenever you bite into your grilled cheese
or your burger, or lick your ice cream cone,
remember that the deliciousness you're tasting
was a gift from the humble cow and the burps of
countless microbes. Like termites and other plant
eaters, cows (or their ancestors, at least) found
out early on in evolutionary history that the
world was covered in grass and leaves. And also
that grass and leaves, using that tough-to-crack

cellulose as their building blocks, were not nutritious. If only these plant eaters could break down cellulose and unlock the meal within! Here come microbes again, the only creatures on the planet with the ability to turn flimsy grass into fuel to power a 1,200-pound (540-kilogram) cow. (Leave it to people to use cows to turn grass, which we still can't digest, into steaks, ice cream, and milkshakes, which we love to digest.)

Turning a field into fuel isn't easy, but cows have four stomachs to do it. Each stomach has a different blend of microbes, including archaea, bacteria, protozoa, and viruses. It takes between one and three days to make this microbial magic happen. Bessie chews the grass to break it up, then swallows it, and the first two stomachs ferment the chewed-up grass, helping to break down the cellulose. Then the cow barfs her ball of half-digested grass, which we ranch hands call "cud," back into her mouth and chews it up again. When the chewing-the-cud part of her digestive routine is finished, she swallows it again, and combinations of different microbes continue the fermenting work (making vitamins, fats, and proteins in the process). As the microbes ferment, they release methane gas as a by-product, which Bessie happily belches out (excuse you!). Eventually, the food passes along to the other two stomachs and on down to the intestines to be ejected as cow poop.

All this to say, simple digestion for a cow is a complicated business.

There's a dark side to our ice cream sandwiches, and it has to do with the methane burps the cows' microbes make. Methane is a greenhouse gas. You know, the stuff that contributes to climate change. You might hear a lot about carbon dioxide from our cars causing damage in the earth's atmosphere, warming the planet, acidifying the oceans, and so on. But methane is twenty-eight times more effective at trapping the heat from the earth than carbon dioxide.

"It's just a cow!" you say? Yes, a cow or two won't change the course of the planet. Giraffes eat leaves, and their microbes make methane, too. The thing is, we eat a lot of hamburgers. Earth has 1.4 *billion* cows belching their way around pastures, and by their powers combined, they contribute up to 40 percent of the world's methane produced. The steaks are high, cows!

Scientists, being scientists, many of whom like mint chocolate chip ice cream very much, want to help stop the methane madness. They studied the

methane poots of each cow microbe and found
that archaea (the single-celled critters)
make the most methane of all. Then the
scientists tried to change the microbe
mix in cow stomachs—less archaea,
more bacteria—to help the cow
make less methane. They fiddled
with the cow's diet, tried to change
the microbes straight in the cow's gut.

"No dice," said the cow and her
microbes. "We like it this way."

So the scientists went deeper and found that
cows with some genes keep more archaea than
cows with other genes. When they bred cows
with genes that don't keep as many methane
makers, the calves harbored less archaea and
so burped less methane. Today, researchers are
working to breed a fleet of archaea-hostile cow
babies to help clear the air. In the meantime,
maybe consider the chicken nuggets or Tofurky
every now and then.

Bacon, Chicken Fingers, and Turkey Dinners

Bacon, chicken fingers, and turkey dinners are some people's delectable dietary staples that come from pigs and fowl, of course. And like our own existence, the very existence of swine and fowl depends on the microbes they breed on and in their bodies. Here are two of our favorite pig-and-poultry microbe stories, in limerick form.

To keep your pig feeling just fine,
its microbes must keep the right time.
To feed it at night
would never be right—
they'd be fast asleep in your swine.

What we're saying here is that much of a pig's microbiome has its own day-night cycle. That is, some microbes are more active in the daytime and others are more active at night. This is the same for us humans, too. And mice, while we're at it. For example, the bacterium *Lactobacillus*, which helps us digest all kinds of food, is more abundant in our bodies when we're resting (which is night-time for most of us and daytime for mice). When you feed pigs, mice, or people at weird times, it can really do a number on digestion.

For birds of the poultry persuasion,

fine dining's no prolonged occasion.

From first bite to poop,

in all manner of coop,

it's speedy by any equation.

Poultry, like turkeys, ducks, and chickens, have really short digestive tracts, so food doesn't spend much time hanging around in their bodies (unlike cows, which, you'll remember, take *days* to digest grass in that whippity-whompity, doodad-packed digestive system of theirs). Because there's not much travel time from eating to the number two side—food moves through birds like it's on the

roller coaster of a lifetime— poultry gut microbes have evolved to hang on tight to the birds' insides, doing their breakneck digestion jobs while being extra clingy to the birds' organs.

When Harry Met Sally: A Story of a Glowing Friendship

Here's a buddy story about two real creeps.
Dreadful, friendly creeps. The first is a nematode (that's a type of worm) called *Heterorhabditis
bacteriophora*. (You can say it if you feel like
it—het-uh-roar-HAB-dit-us back-TEE-ree-oh-
FOR-uh—but let's just call it Harry. No, not

Hairy. That would make no sense. These nematodes are bald.) Harry's beige and about as long as your fingernail is thick. That's pretty small, but you can still see him if you really look, so Harry doesn't count as a microbe. (Harry could be male, female, or both at once, but here we're just saying "he.")

Harry swims through dirt all over the world, in the warmer parts of every continent except Antarctica (which has no warmer parts). When Harry isn't swimming through the soil, he's giving insects the worst day of their lives. You see, Harry needs insects to make lots of baby Harrys. Harry needs the *whole* insect. But compared to Harry, your average insect is ginormous! How can Harry conquer a whole insect, you ask? That's where Harry's best bacterial buddy, *Photorhabdus luminescens*, comes in. Nice to meet you, *Photorhabdiddylblahblahblah*. We'll call her Sally. Sallys aren't male or female.

They're bacteria. But here we're going to say "she" because it makes it easier to tell when we're talking about Harry and when we're talking about Sally.

Sally is tough but delicate. She needs to live inside someone, for someone to carry her from place to place and give her food, or she will die. Harry needs to take down giant insects. To do both these things, they need each other, which is how great friendships are made. Or at least how this very particular friendship is formed.

Sally lives in Harry's little guts. She can't live anywhere else. When Harry swims through the soil, he takes Sally with him. When he pokes his little nematode head out and waits for a bug to come crawling along, Sally waits in his belly. And when Harry launches himself out of the ground, attaches himself to an insect, like a caterpillar, and either swims inside its body through an open hole or hacks his way in using his insect-hacking tooth, Sally prepares to get to work.

Harry swims through the caterpillar, barfing out Sally as he goes. And Sally releases a poison so toxic that ten cells of Sally can kill the caterpillar in less than a day. All the while, both Harry and Sally are eating the caterpillar from the inside out, turning caterpillar cells into Harry and Sally cells. Sally releases another chemical that keeps the dead caterpillar from rotting.

Now, any reasonable bird or frog hopping around that spies a perfectly good caterpillar lying on the ground, completely immobilized, as Harry and Sally's caterpillar would be, would recognize an easy meal when it sees one and chomp it down immediately. That would be bad business for Harry and Sally, who would die in the bird's or frog's digestive tract.

"Don't worry, Harry!" Sally says (if Sally could talk and Harry could worry). "I've got this!"

Sally releases a ton of chemicals that meet the following requirements for Awesome Way Not to Get Eaten:

☑ Makes caterpillar smell especially terrible (Smells gross? Must taste gross!)

☑ Makes caterpillar turn bright red, which is a warning color to stay away

☑ Makes caterpillar GLOW (Yes. Sally makes it glow. This freaks would-be bug snackers out. They leave it alone, as you probably would if your hot dog suddenly started to glow.)

☑ Bonus: Releases special scent to deter scavenging ants

☑ Bonus: Releases special chemicals to kill other nematodes

All the while, Harry swims around in the Sally soup, making more Harrys. There comes a point when so many Harrys fill the body of what used to be a caterpillar, it is now a glowing red, stinky mess. When this happens, together they burst out of the corpse in a wiggling tangle of Harrys. Before each Harry leaves, he swallows a mouthful of Sallys to take with him. After all, they can't live without each other.

"Poor caterpillar! Poor bugs! How do we keep Harry and Sally out of our yards?!" you may exclaim.

We don't. In fact, farmers actually mix up big vats of Harrys and Sallys to spray on their fields. It turns out this relationship works out pretty well for folks tired of battling bugs with human-

made chemicals. Harry and Sally have worked together to save citrus orchards, field crops, and more. And, as we learn more about how to use them, we'll find better ways of keeping them

happy in our farm dirt. This could be the beginning of a beautiful friendship . . .

Nobody Messes with Hamilton

Aphids are the unsung villains of the agricultural world. They're easy to overlook. First, they are tiny, usually about the size of a sesame seed. Second, they're adorable. Aphids have spiderweb-thin legs, little puppy eyes, and giant booties that they often poke up in the air to release their waste, which has the sweet name of honeydew. How bad can something so endearing be? Very.

Even though only 100 or so of the 4,000 aphid species on earth live on our crop plants, they cause major damage to the food we eat. For meals, they sip phloem, or plant juice. They do this by stabbing the plant with mouths that are like sharp straws. When aphids sip phloem, they gulp nutrients that the plant needs to keep itself healthy. Also, when they stab the plant with their needlelike mouths, they can inject diseases into the plant. Their sweet poop is a problem, too, because it accumulates on plants, where it molds and blocks the sun, so the plant can't make energy. The result is a loss of vast quantities of food that we could otherwise eat. In Europe alone, aphids are responsible for the waste of 850,000 tons of potatoes. Let's not dwell on how many french fries and bags of chips that is. It's too sad.

Plenty of aphids have microbes that go to work for them. Phloem isn't super nutritious as a sole food source, so aphids need microbes to make nutrients out of plant juice. But one of the most amazing bonds between aphids and their bacterial buddies is between the pea aphid and a

bacterium called *Hamiltonella defensa* (HAM-ill-
ton-ELL-uh dee-FENS-uh, or Hamilton for short).
Aphid mamas can infect their female babies with
Hamilton; otherwise, these girls have to get it
through mating or being stabbed by a wasp. We'll
come to the stabbed-by-a-wasp part in a second.
Now, Hamilton infects aphids, but Hamilton itself
can get infected by a virus called APSE.

Quick recap: Here's where we are
right now. Pea aphids are tiny insects.
They get infected by the bacterium
we're calling Hamilton. Hamilton gets
infected by the virus APSE. Following
us so far? Let's add someone else into
the mix. A parasitoid wasp.

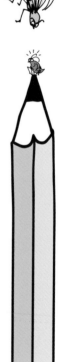

Parasitoids lay their eggs in other
insects by stabbing them with their
pointy egg-laying stingers, called
ovipositors, which inject their eggs
inside the bug. Their eggs hatch and
their larvae swim around the insect's

body, eating it from the inside out, and eventually burst forth as adults to continue the cycle.

Hamilton, who needs pea aphids to survive, isn't going to let anyone mess with his aphid. When wasps lay their eggs in aphids infected with Hamilton, Hamilton's virus APSE makes toxins that target the wasp babies, killing them.

"Nobody tries to hurt Hamilton's aphid!" APSE says as it gives the baby wasps the ole chemical TKO.

Wasp babies can't survive in Hamilton + APSE–infected aphids. To make matters worse for the wasps, would-be wasp mamas pick up Hamilton on their ovipositors when they try to lay their eggs in infected aphids. Their ovipositors get covered with Hamilton and APSE. Then when the wasps fly to uninfected aphids, they spread the wasp-killing microbe team to those aphids, sealing the doom for generations of baby wasps to come. This also spells doom for the crops we eat, because when it comes to getting slurped on by aphids, they'd rather not.

Part IV

You

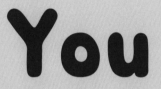

You are what you host—the microbes you host on and in your body, that is. Actually, a lot of your body is made of microbes. Why are they here? What are they doing to us? WHO IS REALLY IN CHARGE?!?! There's only one way to find out.* Turn the page!

---

*Okay, there are plenty of ways to find out. This world is filled with excellent resources to help you find the answers to your questions. Teachers, friends, mentors, bathroom walls, libraries, fortune cookies, the Internet . . . But if you want to know right now about what some microbes are doing on your body, and you're already holding this book in your hands, take it from us: this is your very best option. Go on and turn that page. You'll see.

What About Us? A World of Wonder

Of course dookie-eating flies have microbes! And of course termites need microbes because they eat *wood*, of all things (pass the doughnuts, please). But don't think you're getting off so easy. You are literally *covered* from head to toe in an abundance of life. You are a walking jungle, and a peek inside that jungle reveals *jungles within jungles,* oceans of yeasts, colonies of bacteria shouting chemicals at each other across your forehead. In addition to harvesting microbes from your mother and your dog, you pick them up from your daily way of life, and your diet helps determine which species can flourish and which get the boot.

Researchers believe that the microbial cells on your body outnumber your human cells at least three to one, and if you managed to evict them all and put them in a pile, they would weigh up to 5 pounds (2.3 kilograms). (That's like a couple of cantaloupes' worth of living beings smeared on and in you.) Your microbiome is as unique as your fingerprint. Without it, you would not be able to digest food properly or keep bad microbial actors from invading your body. Likely, you would become depressed, malnourished, and very sick. And without major medical intervention, eventually you would perish. They are as much a part of you as your cells are. So let's celebrate them!

Here are some of our favorite microbial parties on and in the human body.

Your Head

Mouth: Microbes in here eat your food and drink your drinks. And they cling tight to avoid getting swallowed and killed in your stomach. Some aren't so great, like the group that forms plaque on your teeth.

Ears: Your ears have three sections: outer, middle, and inner. The outer and middle ear host very different microbes from each other; the inner ear is sealed off and virtually microbe-free.

Skin: Your skin is the first defense in your immune system, a barrier to bad guys trying to make their way into your body. One of the most important parts of your skin is your microbial community, which covers nearly every available space, leaving no room for the ruffians to set up shop. In this case, ruffians are microbes that can make us sick, like staph or MRSA. Some skin microbes also fight potential pathogens by

releasing chemicals. Many feast on our sweat and oils.

Forehead: You have mites that live in your hair follicles. At night they crawl around your forehead, searching for mates. You're welcome.

Your Outsides

Armpits: The most famous microbes in our armpits are renowned for giving us our "pit funk" smell, which isn't everyone's favorite perfume these days. But trust us: in the olden days, a ripe pit funk made you suuuper attractive to others.

Feet: Your tootsies, complete with the creases and folds between your toes, have one of the most diverse and abundant microbe populations on your body. Because you use your feet for walking around, they come in contact with all sorts of stuff, picking up microbes along the way. Some of them give you foot odor, and many of them can withstand the sweaty-to-dry-to-sweaty-to-dry wringer you put them through. If you fool around with them too much, they can't protect your feet from some of the nastier creatures that like to set up shop on and between your little piggies. Like toenail fungus. Or bacteria that gobble your skin and cause a condition called pitted keratolysis. Or algae that give you spots and other trouble. And many, many more. Celebrate your stinky feet!

Butt crack: Or what scientists call the "gluteal crease," which is way classier. Try it out on your friends and enemies. You will sound sophisticated and insulting at once when you inform them they can kiss it. Or that they smell like a perspiring one. What were we talking about? Oh, microbes. The ~~butt crack~~ gluteal crease is a sweaty swimming pool for a tremendous number of microbes, some of which come from your poop. They try to clean you up down there and can smell a little funky, too.

Belly button: Your average belly button exists as nice, dark folds. "Thank you for the moist caves!" say your microbes, which flourish there. Your belly button is its very own habitat, harboring up to 200 different types of microbes.

Your Insides

Stomach: Your stomach microbiome has been linked to everything from obesity to diabetes to brain disorders. Stressin' out can alter which species thrive there, as can illness and not eating healthy foods (or enough food, or too much food). Treat that tummy well! It'll give you a big high five!

Intestines: Your first shot of gastrointestinal microbes comes from your mama when she's giving birth to you. If she had a C-section, you didn't get all her microbes, but don't fear. Over time, you built up your own little population. Some microbes in your intestines just hang out, neither helping too much nor hurting anything, as far as we can tell. Others can make us sick if the good guys don't work to keep the sick makers' population low. And other microbes are major helpers, pitching in to digest tough-to-break-down food-stuffs like fiber, or by making things we need, like vitamins K and B. As with our belly microbes, a good diet keeps your intestinal jungle happy. Take care of those innards!

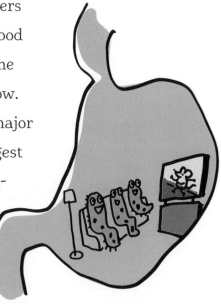

Your Body: Worst-Case Scenarios

Microbes are great! Yay! But some microbes are capable of taking over our bodies and brains on amazingly complicated levels. Here are a couple of worst-case microbial scenarios we hope you never have to encounter.

Mad Dog! Mad Dog!

In most parts of the world, you don't hear people shouting, "Mad dog!" (or "狂犬!" or *"Chien enragé!"* or even *"Galen hund!"*) like you used to. That's because, these days, lots of people can get their pet pups vaccinated against rabies. Remember rabies? The foaming at the mouth, the bleary-eyed insanity, the fear of water, and the bites . . . so . . . much . . . biting . . .

Rabies is one of those worst-case viral mind-control scenarios. Now, remember: we said some folks don't consider viruses to be microbes because viruses don't meet the Official Criteria for Being Alive:

- ? Movement
- X Breathing or respiration
- X Excretion
- ? Growth
- X Sensitivity
- X Reproduction

Still, other researchers say, "We can't see 'em! They affect us! Throw 'em in with the rest of the microbe party!" As such, we present to you RABIES. One party you hope never comes knockin' at your door.

Rabies loves saliva, slobber, spit, drool, and whatever else you call that juicy stuff that comes out of your mouth. It loves saliva because it uses spit to move from animal to animal. Just imagine a tiny rabies virus, 100 times smaller than our human cells, all alone in this world, looking for a friend. (Of course, viruses can't look. They don't have eyes, remember? And really, they don't have brains, so they don't get lonely and don't actually need friends. They mostly are like extremely tiny, extremely deadly robots with one mission: reproduce, reproduce, reproduce. To us, that looks like another mission: kill, kill, kill.)

"I know! I'll make a friend! I'll make millions of friends!" rabies tells itself. "But however will I do this? I kill everyone I meet, and I can't survive outside anyone's body for too long. It's so cold and so dry."

And so begins the virus's rabid mission to make rabies babies (which, if you'll recall, are just identical copies of the virus because viruses don't grow).

The rabies virus (a.k.a. *Rabies lyssavirus*) can live in nearly any mammal, including bats, coyotes, foxes, raccoons, dogs, skunks, and humans. Rabies cannot, however, live very easily in opossums. Opossums have a weirdly low body temperature, too low for many viruses to survive. Opossums are also immune to many snake venoms. Because opossums, though they be ugly, are secretly invincible. Their one weakness? Crossing the street. They have a hard time doing that safely.

Rabies gets into the body of an uninfected animal when an infected animal bites it. For the sake of stinkiness, let's say an infected skunk bites a human girl. The skunk's slobber makes it under the girl's skin, thanks to those pointy little skin-poking skunk teeth. Then the virus travels slooooowly along her nerves to her spinal cord, working its way to the poor girl's brain. Depending on how close the bite is to the brain and how many copies of the virus make it into the girl, this can take ten days, or it can take MONTHS. Can't rush rabies!

Once in her brain, the virus begins to ramp up its mission to make more rabies. Because it causes so much destruction in the brain, it will surely kill the girl. In fact, since the girl didn't realize the skunk had rabies and didn't seek immediate treatment, she has no chance to recover. She will die. Once the virus makes its way to the spinal cord and brain, even with the best medical treatments available today, rabies is not survivable (and kills nearly 60,000 people around the world each year). Therefore, the virus needs to infect another animal so it can continue to copy itself. But how can the virus make the leap from the girl's skull to the body of another animal if it can't survive outside? This is where the mind control comes in.

Rabies hangs out in the spaces between brain cells as it replicates, replicates, replicates. These spaces are kind of like hallways where brain cells holler things at one another, like "Time to do this to keep it all running smoothly!" and "Let's all work together, everybody!" When the virus hangs out in the hallways, it makes the conversations between cells come out a little screwy. Meanwhile, the virus binds to special receptors in other cells that impact the girl's muscle control. She starts acting weird. She gets confused, restless, uncontrollably excited. She can't sleep. She starts to hallucinate.

At this point, the virus has made its way to the girl's salivary glands and starts forcing her to make tons of slobber. The virus in the brain also causes painful spasms in her throat that can be triggered by a tiny breath or swallowing, so the girl becomes terrified of drinking water, or even swallowing all that rabies-packed drool. This extra drool pools and froths in her mouth, and the girl, who we already know is going to die, is 100 percent out of her head, making no sense by now. She lashes out at others because she is afraid and confused. She could even bite someone, though the pre-rabies girl would never consider biting *anyone*. Because the virus spreads through slobber-filled bites, of course it's trying all the tricks in its book to get the girl *to* bite someone. Once she reaches the part where she's afraid of drinking water, she dies within a few days of cardiorespiratory arrest. That means her heart and lungs stop working. The rabies that built up inside her body dies with her. Back in the woods, the sad, rabid skunk has also died, hopefully without biting anyone else.

A Better Mousetrap

One sad fact for the short lives of mice is that good ole snap traps, which have been around for about 130 years, remain one of the most effective  ways to send mice straight to rodent paradise in no time flat. You know, the wooden rectangles with a little spot for cheese or peanut butter to lure the mouse, which thinks it's getting a picnic and instead gets flattened by a spring-loaded whacker. Simple, yet sinister.

But there's one microbe, a tiny creature called a protist, more specifically *Toxoplasma gondii* (TOK-soh-PLAZ-mah GON-dee-eye), that one-ups the snap trap in its mouse-murder effectiveness and blows the snap trap out of the water in the competition for creepy killing methods. The protist uses a weird mix of mind control, bodies, and poop to make it one of the most prevalent infections on the planet. It infects everything from pigs to koalas, otters to pandas, and, yes, humans. Up to a third of all people on earth are infected with *Toxoplasma gondii*, and for some of us, that spells a lifetime of torture. But we'll get to that later. Let's go back to the poopy beginnings.

It all begins with a little doo-doo–eating mouse. *Toxoplasma gondii*, which we're going to call Toxie for short, looks like a fat little boomerang under a very powerful microscope. Because Toxie's a protist, it's a whole animal packed into a cell. It can reproduce asexually (that is, without finding a mate) in all kinds of creatures, but what really gets its motor running is finding a mate and reproducing sexually. The thing is, it can do that only inside the intestines of cats. Imagine now thousands of little Toxies, boomeranging around a cat's intestines, having a big ole ball. But something happens. The cat dies. Then all those Toxies are dead, too. You see, Toxie needs to live in not just one cat, but *many* cats, so that Toxie isn't wiped off the face of the earth when the cat goes splat. The trouble is, Toxie lives in the cat's intestines. It leaves the cat's body when the cat poops. But other cats aren't going to come around to eat that cat's poop. I mean, they spend a large portion of their days—when they're not reminding us how much cooler than us they are—giving themselves baths. These VIP members of Clean Freaks R Us are no feces feasters. But you know what does come in contact with cat poop as they skitter around in the dark? Mice. And you know what cats love to eat? You guessed it.

That's where the diabolical Toxie plan begins to unfold in its awful, twisted way. A mouse runs over some Toxie-infested cat poop, maybe, and licks its paws to clean them. Or say it rained, and the mouse stumbles across some dirt where cat poop was washed about in the rain, spreading Toxies around the ground for the poor mouse to pick up. Either way, once a mouse gets Toxie in its body, Toxie goes to the mouse's brain, and something very strange happens to the mouse. It begins to take risks. Like, instead of hiding behind things, it runs out in the open. And it starts to not be afraid of things that are very important for mice to be afraid of. Like the smell of cat pee. In fact, it starts to be attracted to this surefire signal that a hungry cat's around. That makes it easier for Mr. Sneaky Snickers the Toxie-less cat to pounce and devour his favorite rodent prey.

"This is too good to be true!" Mr. Sneaky Snickers thinks to himself as that poor Toxie-deranged mouse practically wanders between his paws and places its head in his mouth.

Yes, Mr. Sneaky Snickers. It *is* too good to be true. Your intestines are now a hard-cranking Toxie factory. Some cats can get very sick from *Toxoplasma gondii.* Others bop along, pooping out the hard stuff, infecting anyone who grabs it. Including humans.

Toxie doesn't really need humans to complete its life cycle like it needs cats. And you don't hear about too many cats gobbling up their people. But humans can still get infected with the protist, and sometimes it can cause big problems. Remember, nearly one out of every three people in the world is infected with *Toxoplasma gondii,* and in some places, six out of every ten people have the protist swimming around their brains. They can pick it up without knowing it, like when they clean out the litter box or harvest vegetables from soil where Mr. Sneaky Snickers had a secret BM. Or when they eat undercooked meat from infected animals, like cows, chicken, and pigs.

Many infected people never know that they have an abundance of protists forming tiny cysts in their brains. But for some people infected by Toxie, those cysts can be devastating. That same reckless behavior experienced by mice takes new forms in humans. People infected with Toxie have a higher likelihood of getting in car crashes. People with schizophrenia also are more likely to have the protist living in their bodies. When infected pregnant people accidentally pass the protist to their unborn babies, those babies could have deafness, seizures, or intellectual disabilities. Sometimes, the babies can die.

Strangely enough, infected people also have changes in their response to cat odors, reporting them as less noxious than the rest of us. But why? Is it one great microbial plot to destroy us?

Have Toxies and cats teamed up so cats may take what they feel is their rightful place as our over-lords? If so, they've been working on this plan for a long, long time. Like, tens of thousands of years. Still, cats are patient creatures. They can wait . . .

But Wait! There's More!

Can't get enough microbes? Here are some places to go and things to do to feed your microbial curiosity.

Want to read more about microbes?

First, if you are considering working with microbes as a job, you may want to be a microbiologist. Which means you would like to learn about microbiology. Simon Basher and Dan Green's *Microbiology: It's a Small World!* is here to get you rolling.

For the hands-on learner: If you're ready for some at-home microbe projects, check out Christine Burillo-Kirch and Tom Casteel's

Microbes: Discover an Unseen World, which features twenty-five fun experiments you can do to investigate microbes on your own. There's even a whole coloring book about microbes called *Virus Adult Coloring Book of Germs, Bacteria, Microbes* by Alina Zoll.

If you want your parents to read something cool about microbes, tell them to check out Ed Yong's *I Contain Multitudes: The Microbes Within Us and a Grander View of Life,* which shares tales of the mysterious and wonderful work microbes are doing on and in you.

Want to do some actual scientific microbe research from the comfort of your home (or yard or classroom)?

You'll be a great citizen scientist! A citizen scientist is a person who helps contribute data to real scientific studies. Scientists sometimes ask questions that they need a lot of help answering. Help from YOU. At **zooniverse.org** and **scistarter.org**, your input makes a difference. From microbes to animal behavior to Egyptology, these folks have your scientific curiosity covered. Try helping out with one of their studies! You'll like it! And if you don't like it, try another study!

Want to draw the microbe *E. coli* enjoying a hot dog?

You're in luck. Rob Wilson's going to show you how.

Escherichia coli (called *E. coli* by its friends) is a bacterial microbe that lives on and in all sorts of creatures, including your intestines. Many types of *E. coli* are harmless (you probably didn't even know they were there!), but some'll make you really sick. Like throw-up-and-the-runs sick. This little guy down here won't make you sick. It really loves its hot dog.

First

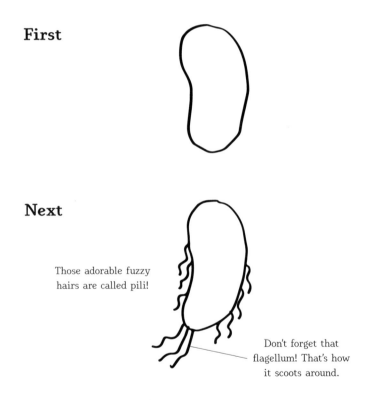

Next

Those adorable fuzzy hairs are called pili!

Don't forget that flagellum! That's how it scoots around.

Then

E. coli doesn't really have eyes. Or a mouth. Or arms. But they are fun to draw.

Finally

"That's one good dog!"

Feel free to add your own toppings.

Don't stop now!

If you want to check out some of the research the scientists did to find out all this cool stuff, you can visit their labs' websites or read the actual, real-live studies! Turn the page to find a bunch of those studies that we used to tell you stories about microbes.

Bibliography

Part I: House

Flight of the Living Dead

Brobyn, Patricia J., and N. Wilding. "Invasive and Developmental Processes of *Entomophthora muscae* Infecting Houseflies (*Musca domestica*)." *Transactions of the British Mycological Society* 80, no. 1 (1983): 1–8. https://doi.org/10.1016/S0007-1536(83)80157-0.

Junqueira, Ana Carolina M., Aakrosh Ratan, Enzo Acerbi, et al. "The Microbiomes of Blowflies and Houseflies as Bacterial Transmission Reservoirs." *Scientific Reports* 7, article no. 16324 (2017). https://doi.org/10.1038/s41598-017-16353-x.

Krasnoff, S. B., D. W. Watson, D. M. Gibson, and E. C. Kwan. "Behavioral Effects of the Entomopathogenic Fungus, *Entomophthora muscae* on Its Host *Musca domestica*: Postural Changes in Dying Hosts and Gated Pattern of Mortality." *Journal of Insect Physiology* 41, no. 10 (1995): 895–903. https://doi.org/10.1016/0022-1910(95)00026-Q.

Park, Rahel, Maria C. Dzialo, Stijn Spaepen, et al. "Microbial Communities of the House Fly *Musca domestica* Vary with Geographical Location and Habitat." *Microbiome* 7, article no. 147 (2019). https://doi.org/10.1186/s40168-019-0748-9.

Watson, D. W., B. A. Mullens, and J. J. Petersen. "Behavioral Fever Response of *Musca domestica* (Diptera: Muscidae) to Infection by *Entomophthora muscae* (Zygomycetes: Entomophthorales)." *Journal of Invertebrate Pathology* 61, no. 1 (1993): 10–16. https://doi.org/10.1006/jipa.1993.1003.

Buttfiti

Bermingham, Emma N., Wayne Young, Christina F. Butowski, et al. "The Fecal Microbiota in the Domestic Cat (*Felis catus*) Is Influenced by Interactions between Age and Diet; A Five Year Longitudinal Study." *Frontiers in Microbiology* (2018). https://doi.org/10.3389/fmicb.2018.01231.

Older, Caitlin E., Alison B. Diesel, Sara D. Lawhon, Cintia R. R. Queiroz, Luan C. Henker, and Aline Rodrigues Hoffmann. "The Feline Cutaneous and

Oral Microbiota Are Influenced by Breed and Environment." *PLOS ONE* (2019). https://doi.org/10.1371/journal.pone.0220463.

Yamaguchi, Mei S., Holly H. Ganz, Adrienne W. Cho, et al. "Bacteria Isolated from Bengal Cat (*Felis catus* × *Prionailurus bengalensis*) Anal Sac Secretions Produce Volatile Compounds Potentially Associated with Animal Signaling." *PLOS ONE* (2019). https://doi.org/10.1371/journal.pone.0216846.

The Diggity on Dogs

Do, Sungho, Thunyaporn Phungviwatnikul, Maria R. C. de Godoy, and Kelly S. Swanson. "Nutrient Digestibility and Fecal Characteristics, Microbiota, and Metabolites in Dogs Fed Human-Grade Foods." *Journal of Animal Science* 99, no. 2 (2021). https://doi.org/10.1093/jas/skab028.

Gupta, Sujata. "Microbiome: Puppy Power." *Nature* 543, no. S48–S49 (2017). https://doi.org/10.1038/543S48a.

Hakanen, Emma, Jenni Lehtimäki, Elina Salmela, et al. "Urban Environment Predisposes Dogs and Their Owners to Allergic Symptoms." *Scientific Reports* 8, article no. 1585 (2018). https://doi.org/10.1038/s41598-018-19953-3.

Lallensack, Rachael. "Ancient Genomes Heat Up Dog Domestication Debate." *Nature* (2017). https://doi.org/10.1038/nature.2017.22320.

Song, Se Jin, Christian Lauber, Elizabeth K. Costello, et al. "Cohabiting Family Members Share Microbiota with One Another and with Their Dogs." *eLife* 2 (2013). https://doi.org/10.7554/eLife.00458.

Keep Your Pets Close and Your Microbes Closer

Marrs, Tom, Kirsty Logan, Joanna Craven, et al. "Dog Ownership at Three Months of Age Is Associated with Protection against Food Allergy." *Allergy* 74, no. 11 (2019): 2212–2219. https://doi.org/10.1111/all.13868.

Tun, Hein M., Theodore Konya, Tim K. Takaro, et al. "Exposure to Household Furry Pets Influences the Gut Microbiota of Infants at 3–4 Months following Various Birth Scenarios." *Microbiome* 5, article no. 40 (2017). https://doi.org/10.1186/s40168-017-0254-x.

Don't Approach the Roach

Akbar, N., R. Siddiqui, M. Iqbal, K. Sagathevan, and N. A. Khan. "Gut Bacteria of Cockroaches Are a Potential Source of Antibacterial Compound(s)." *Letters*

in Applied Microbiology 66, no. 5 (2018): 416–426. https://doi.org/10.1111
/lam.12867.

Beccaloni, George, and Paul Eggleton. "Order Blattodea." *Zootaxa* 3703, no. 1
(2013). https://doi.org/10.11646/zootaxa.3703.1.10.

Jahnes, Benjamin C., and Zakee L. Sabree. "Nutritional Symbiosis and Ecology
of Host-Gut Microbe Systems in the Blattodea." *Current Opinion in Insect
Science* 39 (2020): 35–41. https://doi.org/10.1016/j.cois.2020.01.001.

Noda, Tomohito, Genta Okude, Xian-Ying Meng, Ryuichi Koga, Minoru Mori-
yama, and Takema Fukatsu. "Bacteriocytes and Blattabacterium Endosym-
bionts of the German Cockroach *Blattella germanica*, the Forest Cockroach
Blattella nipponica, and Other Cockroach Species." *Zoological Science* 37, no. 5
(2020): 399–410. https://doi.org/10.2108/zs200054.

Pietri, Jose E., Connor Tiffany, and Dangsheng Liang. "Disruption of the
Microbiota Affects Physiological and Evolutionary Aspects of Insecticide
Resistance in the German Cockroach, an Important Urban Pest." *PLOS ONE*
(2018). https://doi.org/10.1371/journal.pone.0207985.

Sacchi, L., C. A. Nalepa, M. Lenz, et al. "Transovarial Transmission of
Symbiotic Bacteria in *Mastotermes darwiniensis* (Isoptera: Mastotermit-
idae): Ultrastructural Aspects and Phylogenetic Implications." *Annals of the
Entomological Society of America* 93, no. 6 (2000): 1308–1313. https://doi
.org/10.1603/0013-8746(2000)093[1308:TTOSBI]2.0.CO;2.

Fart as if the Future of the Human Race Depended on It

Bourguignon, Thomas, Nathan Lo, Carsten Dietrich, et al. "Rampant Host
Switching Shaped the Termite Gut Microbiome." *Current Biology* 28, no. 4
(2018). https://doi.org/10.1016/j.cub.2018.01.035.

Brune, Andreas. "Symbiotic Digestion of Lignocellulose in Termite Guts."
Nature Reviews Microbiology 12 (2014): 168–180. https://doi.org/10.1038
/nrmicro3182.

Matsumoto, Tadao, and Takuya Abe. "The Role of Termites in an Equatorial
Rain Forest Ecosystem of West Malaysia." *Oecologia* 38 (1979): 261–274.
https://doi.org/10.1007/BF00345187.

Nalepa, C. A., D. E. Bignell, and C. Bandi. "Detritivory, Coprophagy, and the
Evolution of Digestive Mutualisms in Dictyoptera." *Insectes Sociaux* 48
(2001): 194–201. https://doi.org/10.1007/PL00001767.

Nauer, Philipp A., Lindsay B. Hutley, and Stefan K. Arndt. "Termite Mounds Mitigate Half of Termite Methane Emissions." *Proceedings of the National Academy of Sciences* 115, no. 52 (2018): 13306–13311. https://doi.org/10.1073/pnas.1809790115.

Ni, Jinfeng, and Gaku Tokuda. "Lignocellulose-Degrading Enzymes from Termites and Their Symbiotic Microbiota." *Biotechnology Advances* 31, no. 6 (2013): 838–850. https://doi.org/10.1016/j.biotechadv.2013.04.005.

Sleep Tight, Don't Let 'Em Bite!

Bellinvia, Sara, Paul R. Johnston, Susan Mbedi, and Oliver Otti. "Mating Changes the Genital Microbiome in Both Sexes of the Common Bedbug *Cimex lectularius* across Populations." *Proceedings of the Royal Society B* 287, no. 1926 (2020). https://doi.org/10.1098/rspb.2020.0302.

Delaunay, Pascal, Véronique Blanc, Pascal Del Giudice, et al. "Bedbugs and Infectious Diseases." *Clinical Infectious Diseases* 52, no. 2 (2011): 200–210. https://doi.org/10.1093/cid/ciq102.

Kakumanu, Madhavi L., Zachary C. DeVries, Alexis M. Barbarin, Richard G. Santangelo, and Coby Schal. "Bed Bugs Shape the Indoor Microbial Community Composition of Infested Homes." *Science of the Total Environment* 743 (2020). https://doi.org/10.1016/j.scitotenv.2020.140704.

Pietri, Jose E., and Dangsheng Liang. "Insecticidal Activity of Doxycycline against the Common Bedbug." *Antimicrobial Agents and Chemotherapy* 64, no. 5 (2020). https://doi.org/10.1128/AAC.00005-20.

Ridge, Gale E., Wade Elmer, Stephanie Gaines, et al. "Xenointoxication of a Rabbit for the Control of the Common Bed Bug *Cimex lectularius* L. Using Ivermectin." *Scientifica* (2019). https://doi.org/10.1155/2019/4793569.

Part II: Yard

Far-Out Cicadas

Cooley, John R., David C. Marshall, and Kathy B. R. Hill. "A Specialized Fungal Parasite (*Massospora cicadina*) Hijacks the Sexual Signals of Periodical Cicadas (Hemiptera: Cicadidae: *Magicicada*)." *Scientific Reports* 8, article no. 1432 (2018). https://doi.org/10.1038/s41598-018-19813-0.

Sanborn, Allen F., and Polly K. Phillips. "Scaling of Sound Pressure Level and Body Size in Cicadas (Homoptera: Cicadidae; Tibicinidae)." *Annals of the Entomological Society of America* 88, no. 4 (1995): 479–484. https://doi.org /10.1093/aesa/88.4.479.

Don't Tell Mom the Babysitter's (Almost) Dead

Dheilly, Nolwenn M., Fanny Maure, Marc Ravallec, et al. "Who Is the Puppet Master? Replication of a Parasitic Wasp–Associated Virus Correlates with Host Behaviour Manipulation." *Proceedings of the Royal Society B* 282, no. 1803 (2015). https://doi.org/10.1098/rspb.2014.2773.

Libersat, Frederic, Maayan Kaiser, and Stav Emanuel. "Mind Control: How Parasites Manipulate Cognitive Functions in Their Insect Hosts." *Frontiers in Psychology* 9 (2018). https://doi.org/10.3389/fpsyg.2018.00572.

Beauty Secrets of Birds

Whittaker, Danielle J., and Kevin R. Theis. "Bacterial Communities Associated with Junco Preen Glands: Preliminary Ramifications for Chemical Signaling." In *Chemical Signals in Vertebrates* 13, edited by Bruce A. Schulte, Thomas E. Goodwin, and Michael H. Ferkin, 105–117. Springer, Cham, 2016. https:// doi.org/10.1007/978-3-319-22026-0_8.

——, Samuel P. Slowinski, Jonathan M. Greenberg, et al. "Experimental Evidence That Symbiotic Bacteria Produce Chemical Cues in a Songbird." *Journal of Experimental Biology* 222, no. 20 (2019). https://doi.org/10.1242 /jeb.202978.

Microbes Trick the Deadliest Animal

Beckmann, John F., Judith A. Ronau, and Mark Hochstrasser. "A *Wolbachia* Deubiquitylating Enzyme Induces Cytoplasmic Incompatibility." *Nature Microbiology* 2, article no. 17007 (2017). https://doi.org/10.1038/nmicrobiol .2017.7.

De Moraes, Consuelo M., Nina M. Stanczyk, Heike S. Betz, et al. "Malaria-Induced Changes in Host Odors Enhance Mosquito Attraction." *Proceedings of the National Academy of Sciences* 111, no. 30 (2014): 11079–11084. https:// doi.org/10.1073/pnas.1405617111.

Gomes, Fabio M., and Carolina Barillas-Mury. "Infection of Anopheline Mosquitoes with *Wolbachia*: Implications for Malaria Control." *PLOS Pathogens* (2018). https://doi.org/10.1371/journal.ppat.1007333.

Mousson, Laurence, Karima Zouache, Camilo Arias-Goeta, Vincent Raquin, Patrick Mavingui, and Anna-Bella Failloux. "The Native *Wolbachia* Symbionts Limit Transmission of Dengue Virus in *Aedes albopictus*." *PLOS Neglected Tropical Diseases* (2012). https://doi.org/10.1371/journal.pntd.0001989.

Smallegange, Renate C., Geert-Jan van Gemert, Marga van de Vegte-Bolmer, et al. "Malaria Infected Mosquitoes Express Enhanced Attraction to Human Odor." *PLOS ONE* 8, no. 5 (2013). https://doi.org/10.1371/journal.pone.0063602.

How to Discover the Big Deal of Little Things

Doremus, Matthew R., Corinne M. Stouthamer, Suzanne E. Kelly, Stephan Schmitz-Esser, and Martha S. Hunter. "*Cardinium* Localization during Its Parasitoid Wasp Host's Development Provides Insights into Cytoplasmic Incompatibility." *Frontiers in Microbiology* 11, article no. 606399 (2020). https://doi.org/10.3389/fmicb.2020.606399.

Gebiola, Marco, Massimo Giorgini, Suzanne E. Kelly, Matthew R. Doremus, Patrick M. Ferree, and Martha S. Hunter. "Cytological Analysis of Cytoplasmic Incompatibility Induced by *Cardinium* Suggests Convergent Evolution with Its Distant Cousin *Wolbachia*." *Proceedings of the Royal Society B* 284, no. 1862 (2017). https://doi.org/10.1098/rspb.2017.1433.

Hagler, James R., and Charles G. Jackson. "Methods for Marking Insects: Current Techniques and Future Prospects." *Annual Review of Entomology* 46 (2001): 511–543. https://doi.org/10.1146/annurev.ento.46.1.511.

White, J. A., S. E. Kelly, S. J. Perlman, and M. S. Hunter. "Cytoplasmic Incompatibility in the Parasitic Wasp *Encarsia inaron*: Disentangling the Roles of *Cardinium* and *Wolbachia* Symbionts." *Heredity* 102 (2009): 483–489. https://doi.org/10.1038/hdy.2009.5.

The Very (Very) Hungry Caterpillar

Park, Eun Ju, Chih-Ming Yin, and John P. Burand. "Baculovirus Replication

Alters Hormone-Regulated Host Development." *Journal of General Virology* 77, no. 3 (1996). https://doi.org/10.1099/0022-1317-77-3-547.

Ruiu, Luca, Roberto Mannu, Maurizio Olivieri, and Andrea Lentini. "Gypsy Moth Management with LdMNPV Baculovirus in Cork Oak Forest." *Forests* 12, no. 4 (2021). https://doi.org/10.3390/f12040495.

Yendol, William G., Robert C. Hedlund, and Franklin B. Lewis. "Field Investigation of a Baculovirus of the Gypsy Moth." *Journal of Economic Entomology* 70, no. 5 (1977). https://doi.org/10.1093/jee/70.5.598.

The Woman Who Gave Caterpillars Poop Transplants

Harris, Erica V., Jacobus C. de Roode, and Nicole M. Gerardo. "Diet–Microbiome–Disease: Investigating Diet's Influence on Infectious Disease Resistance through Alteration of the Gut Microbiome." *PLOS Pathogens* (2019). https://doi.org/10.1371/journal.ppat.1007891.

Bring Out the Dead

Crippen, Tawni L., M. Eric Benbow, and Jennifer L. Pechal. "Chapter 3: Microbial Interactions during Carrion Decomposition." In *Carrion Ecology, Evolution, and Their Applications*, edited by M. Eric Benbow, Jeffery K. Tomberlin, and Aaron M. Tarone. Boca Raton, FL: CRC Press, 2015. https://doi.org/10.1201/b18819.

Roggenbuck, Michael, Ida B. Schnell, Nikolaj Blom, et al. "The Microbiome of New World Vultures." *Nature Communications* 5, article no. 5498 (2014). https://doi.org/10.1038/ncomms6498.

Part III: Food

Bee-youtiful Bee Bowels

Koch, Hauke, and Paul Schmid-Hempel. "Socially Transmitted Gut Microbiota Protect Bumble Bees against an Intestinal Parasite." *Proceedings of the National Academy of Sciences* 108, no. 48 (2011): 19288–19292. https://doi.org/10.1073/pnas.1110474108.

Kwong, Waldan K., and Nancy A. Moran. "Gut Microbial Communities of

Social Bees." *Nature Reviews Microbiology* 14 (2016): 374–384. https://doi
.org/10.1038/nrmicro.2016.43.

Martinson, Vincent G., Jamie Moy, and Nancy A. Moran. "Establishment of
Characteristic Gut Bacteria during Development of the Honeybee Worker."
Applied and Environmental Microbiology 78, no. 8 (2012): 2830–2840.
https://doi.org/10.1128/AEM.07810-11.

Raymann, Kasie, Zack Shaffer, and Nancy A. Moran. "Antibiotic Exposure
Perturbs the Gut Microbiota and Elevates Mortality in Honeybees." *PLOS
Biology* (2017). https://doi.org/10.1371/journal.pbio.2001861.

CoffeeBeetleDon'tQuitWon'tQuit

Acuña, Ricardo, Beatriz E. Padilla, Claudia P. Flórez-Ramos, et al. "Adaptive
Horizontal Transfer of a Bacterial Gene to an Invasive Insect Pest of Coffee."
Proceedings of the National Academy of Sciences 109, no. 11 (2012): 4197–
4202. https://doi.org/10.1073/pnas.1121190109.

Ceja-Navarro, Javier A., Fernando E. Vega, Ulas Karaoz, et al. "Gut Microbiota Mediate Caffeine Detoxification in the Primary Insect Pest of Coffee."
Nature Communications 6, article no. 7618 (2015). https://doi.org/10.1038
/ncomms8618.

Spying on Food Microbes Is a Real Job

McCullum, Nakieta M. "Behavior of *Escherichia coli* O157:H7 on Lettuce and
Spinach and *Salmonella* Montevideo on Tomatoes." Master's thesis, University of Georgia, 2009. https://getd.libs.uga.edu/pdfs/mccullum_nakieta_m
_200905_ms.pdf.

Rootin' Tootin' High Pollutin'

Li, Fuyong, Changxi Li, Yanhong Chen, et al. "Host Genetics Influence the
Rumen Microbiota and Heritable Rumen Microbial Features Associate with
Feed Efficiency in Cattle." *Microbiome* 7, article no. 92 (2019). https://doi
.org/10.1186/s40168-019-0699-1.

Roehe, Rainer, Richard J. Dewhurst, Carol-Anne Duthie, et al. "Bovine Host
Genetic Variation Influences Rumen Microbial Methane Production with
Best Selection Criterion for Low Methane Emitting and Efficiently Feed

Converting Hosts Based on Metagenomic Gene Abundance." *PLOS Genetics* (2016). https://doi.org/10.1371/journal.pgen.1005846.

Wallace, R. John, John A. Rooke, Carol-Anne Duthie, et al. "Archaeal Abundance in Post-Mortem Ruminal Digesta May Help Predict Methane Emissions from Beef Cattle." *Scientific Reports* 4, article no. 5892 (2014). https://doi.org/10.1038/srep05892.

Weimer, P. J., D. M. Stevenson, H. C. Mantovani, and S. L. C. Man. "Host Specificity of the Ruminal Bacterial Community in the Dairy Cow following Near-Total Exchange of Ruminal Contents." *Journal of Dairy Science* 93, no. 12 (2010). https://doi.org/10.3168/jds.2010-3500.

Bacon, Chicken Fingers, and Turkey Dinners

Pan, Deng, and Zhongtang Yu. "Intestinal Microbiome of Poultry and Its Interaction with Host and Diet." *Gut Microbes* 5, no. 1 (2014). https://doi.org/10.4161/gmic.26945.

Parkar, Shanthi G., Andres Kalsbeek, and James F. Cheeseman. "Potential Role for the Gut Microbiota in Modulating Host Circadian Rhythms and Metabolic Health." *Microorganisms* 7, no. 2 (2019). https://doi.org/10.3390/microorganisms7020041.

Van Erp, Rik J. J., Sonja de Vries, Theo A. T. G. van Kempen, Leo A. Den Hartog, and Walter J. J. Gerrits. "Circadian Misalignment Imposed by Nocturnal Feeding Tends to Increase Fat Deposition in Pigs." *British Journal of Nutrition* 123, no. 5 (2019): 529–536. https://doi.org/10.1017/S0007114519003052.

Zarrinpar, Amir, Amandine Chaix, Shibu Yooseph, and Satchidananda Panda. "Diet and Feeding Pattern Affect the Diurnal Dynamics of the Gut Microbiome." *Cell Metabolism* 20, no. 6 (2014): 1006–1017. https://doi.org/10.1016/j.cmet.2014.11.008.

When Harry Met Sally: A Story of a Glowing Friendship

Fenton, Andy, Lucy Magoolagana, Zara Kennedy, and Karen A. Spencer. "Parasite-Induced Warning Coloration: A Novel Form of Host Manipulation." *Animal Behaviour* 81, no. 2 (2011): 417–422. https://doi.org/10.1016/j.anbehav.2010.11.010.

Jones, Rebecca S., Andy Fenton, and Michael P. Speed. "'Parasite-Induced Aposematism' Protects Entomopathogenic Nematode Parasites against Invertebrate Enemies." *Behavioral Ecology* 27, no. 2 (2016): 645–651. https://doi.org/10.1093/beheco/arv202.

Lacey, Lawrence A., and Ramon Georgis. "Entomopathogenic Nematodes for Control of Insect Pests Above and Below Ground with Comments on Commercial Production." *Journal of Nematology* 44, no. 2 (2012): 218–225. https://www.ncbi.nlm.nih.gov/pmc/articles/PMC3578470/.

Waterfield, Nick R., Todd Ciche, and David Clarke. "*Photorhabdus* and a Host of Hosts." *Annual Review of Microbiology* 63 (2009): 557–574. https://doi.org/10.1146/annurev.micro.091208.073507.

Nobody Messes with Hamilton

Oliver, Kerry M., and Clesson H. V. Higashi. "Variations on a Protective Theme: *Hamiltonella defensa* Infections in Aphids Variably Impact Parasitoid Success." *Current Opinion in Insect Science* 32 (2019): 1–7. https://doi.org/10.1016/j.cois.2018.08.009.

Oliver, Kerry M., Patrick H. Degnan, Martha S. Hunter, and Nancy A. Moran. "Bacteriophages Encode Factors Required for Protection in a Symbiotic Mutualism." *Science* 325, no. 5943 (2009): 992–994. https://doi.org/10.1126/science.1174463.

Part IV: You

What About Us? A World of Wonder

Your Head

Grice, Elizabeth A., and Julia A. Segre. "The Skin Microbiome." *Nature Reviews Microbiology* 9 (2011): 244–253. https://doi.org/10.1038/nrmicro2537.

Jervis-Bardy, Jake, Lex E. X. Leong, Lito E. Papanicolas, et al. "Examining the Evidence for an Adult Healthy Middle Ear Microbiome." *mSphere* 4, no. 5 (2019). https://doi.org/10.1128/mSphere.00456-19.

Lousada, M. B., T. Lachnit, J. Edelkamp, et al. "Exploring the Human Hair Follicle Microbiome." *British Journal of Dermatology* 184, no. 5 (2021): 802–815. https://doi.org/10.1111/bjd.19461.

Mullen, Gary R., and Barry M. O'Connor. "Chapter 26 - Mites (Acari)." In *Medical and Veterinary Entomology*, edited by Gary R. Mullen and Lance A. Durden. 3rd ed., 533–602. London: Academic Press, 2019. https://doi.org /10.1016/B978-0-12-814043-7.00026-1.

Segata, Nicola, Susan K. Haake, Peter Mannon, et al. "Composition of the Adult Digestive Tract Bacterial Microbiome Based on Seven Mouth Surfaces, Tonsils, Throat and Stool Samples." *Genome Biology* 13, article no. R42 (2012). https://doi.org/10.1186/gb-2012-13-6-r42.

Your Outsides

Adamczyk, Katarzyna, Agnieszka Garncarczyk, Pawel Antończak, and Dominika Wcisło-Dziadecka. "The Foot Microbiome." *Journal of Cosmetic Dermatology* 19, no. 5 (2020): 1039–1043. https://doi.org/10.1111/jocd .13368.

Dunn, Robert R., Katherine R. Amato, Elizabeth A. Archie, Mimi Arandjelovic, Alyssa N. Crittenden, and Lauren M. Nichols. "The Internal, External and Extended Microbiomes of Hominins." *Frontiers in Ecology and Evolution* 8 (2020). https://doi.org/10.3389/fevo.2020.00025.

Grice, Elizabeth A., and Julia A. Segre. "The Skin Microbiome." *Nature Reviews Microbiology* 9 (2011): 244–253. https://doi.org/10.1038 /nrmicro2537.

Hulcr, Jiri, Andrew M. Latimer, Jessica B. Henley, et al. "A Jungle in There: Bacteria in Belly Buttons Are Highly Diverse, but Predictable." *PLOS ONE* 7, no. 11 (2012). https://doi.org/10.1371/journal.pone.0047712.

Leyden, James J., Kenneth J. McGinley, Erhard Hölzle, John N. Labows, and Albert M. Kligman. "The Microbiology of the Human Axilla and Its Relationship to Axillary Odor." *Journal of Investigative Dermatology* 77, no. 5 (1981): 413–416. https://doi.org/10.1111/1523-1747.ep12494624.

Your Insides

Gilbert, Scott F. "A Holobiont Birth Narrative: The Epigenetic Transmission of the Human Microbiome." *Frontiers in Genetics* (2014). https://doi.org/10 .3389/fgene.2014.00282.

Stearns, Jennifer C., Michael D. J. Lynch, Dilani B. Senadheera, et al. "Bacterial Biogeography of the Human Digestive Tract." *Scientific Reports* 1, article no. 170 (2011). https://doi.org/10.1038/srep00170.

Your Body: Worst-Case Scenarios

Mad Dog! Mad Dog!

Hemachudha, Thiravat, Gabriella Ugolini, Supaporn Wacharapluesadee, Witaya Sungkarat, Shanop Shuangshoti, and Jiraporn Laothamatas. "Human Rabies: Neuropathogenesis, Diagnosis, and Management." *The Lancet Neurology* 12, no. 5 (2013). https://doi.org/10.1016/S1474-4422(13)70038-3.

Rupprecht, Charles E., Cathleen A. Hanlon, and Thiravat Hemachudha. "Rabies Re-examined." *The Lancet Infectious Diseases* 2, no. 6 (2002): 327–343. https://doi.org/10.1016/S1473-3099(02)00287-6.

A Better Mousetrap

Flegr, Jaroslav, Pavlína Lenochová, Zdeněk Hodný, and Marta Vondrová. "Fatal Attraction Phenomenon in Humans: Cat Odour Attractiveness Increased for *Toxoplasma*-Infected Men While Decreased for Infected Women." *PLOS Neglected Tropical Diseases* 5, no. 11 (2011). https://doi.org/10.1371/journal.pntd.0001389.

McAuley, James B. "Congenital Toxoplasmosis." *Journal of the Pediatric Infectious Diseases Society* 3, suppl. 1 (2014): S30–S35. https://doi.org/10.1093/jpids/piu077.

Salviz, Mehti, Jose G. Montoya, Joseph B. Nadol, and Felipe Santos. "Otopathology in Congenital Toxoplasmosis." *Otology & Neurotology* 34, no. 6 (2013): 1165–1169. https://doi.org/10.1097/MAO.0b013e31828297b6.

Webster, Joanne P. "Rats, Cats, People and Parasites: The Impact of Latent Toxoplasmosis on Behaviour." *Microbes and Infection* 3, no. 12 (2001): 1037–1045. https://doi.org/10.1016/S1286-4579(01)01459-9.

Acknowledgments

This text was developed with support from a collaborative research grant—"Collaborative Research: The Saboteur's Tools: Mechanisms for Host Reproductive Manipulation by the Bacterial Arthropod Endosymbiont *Cardinium hertigii*"—to Manuel Kleiner (NSF IOS-2003107), Stephan Schmitz-Esser (NSF IOS-2002987), and Molly Hunter (NSF IOS-2002934).

Thank you, Robin Sutton Anders, for your skillful, sharp, and insightful edits. Thank you to Kirsten Keleher, who provided extensive research for the text, to Julia Ellis, who has a deft eagle eye, and to our agent, Gillian MacKenzie.

Our appreciation goes to the awesome scientists who shared their work with us, including Nakieta McCullum, Erica Harris, Hein Min Tun, and Molly Hunter.

Eleanor would like to thank Greg Rice.

Thank you also to Hilary Van Dusen for recognizing the value of weird microbes and for your perceptive guidance.